GAMES
DIVORCED PEOPLE
PLAY

GAMES DIVORCED PEOPLE PLAY

Dr. Melvyn A. Berke
and
Joanne B. Grant

Prentice-Hall, Inc.
Englewood Cliffs, N.J.

Prentice-Hall International, Inc., *London*
Prentice-Hall of Australia, Pty. Ltd., *Sydney*
Prentice-Hall of Canada, Ltd., *Toronto*
Prentice-Hall of India Private Ltd., *New Delhi*
Prentice-Hall of Japan, Inc., *Tokyo*
Prentice-Hall of Southeast Asia Pte. Ltd., *Singapore*
Whitehall Books, Ltd., *Wellington, New Zealand*

Reward Edition . . . . . . March 1983

Library of Congress Cataloging in Publication Data

Berke, Melvyn A
    Games divorced people play.
    Includes index.
    1. Divorcees--Psychology. I. Grant, Joanne,
        -joint author. II. Title.
HQ814.B6   306.8'9   80-23309

Printed in the United States of America

A WORD
FROM THE AUTHORS

For most of us divorce is hard, painful, anguishing work. The sense of loss, the attempt to cope, and the restructuring of old lives into new identities are frightening and difficult. The fantasies of what we should or shouldn't have done, could have done or would like to have done, tear at our hearts and minds. If we allow it, the "have we done it rights" can eat away at our very fiber.

In the beginning our job is to survive long enough to put the pieces back together in a different, yet whole, happy and meaningful way.

This book doesn't give all the answers; in fact, it probably raises more questions than it gives solutions to. What it does is give you a slice of divorced life and a look at the many pitfalls you can fall into and hopefully avoid.

DIVORCE GAMES

Divorce games are marital games in disguise. They are based on the same needs and wants which led you to marry, separate and divorce. This is why you so often hear, "You're divorced, why are you still doing that?" or "You're stupid to feel that way." You agree, but feel a push to do it anyway.

Danny is an example of just such a problem. He was handsome and adventurous, with the same devilish twinkle in his eyes as his high spirited mother. In 1958, his future seemed secure: he had good looks, was intelligent, had wealthy parents, a zest for life and the choice of whatever girl he wished. He was the kind of guy who could have several beers yet drive the mountain roads as if they were the Indianapolis Speedway, or ski the slopes at breakneck speeds only to walk away with a hearty laugh and yearn for more.

The contrast between Danny's parents was striking. His father was a cold, isolating, controlling man, whose life left little room for laughter. Danny, on the other hand, took after his vivacious, fun loving mother. When he got into skirmishes with the law or with outraged fathers venting their wrath for his trifling with their daughters at the local "passion pit," his father issued a stern reprimand while his mother voiced a sly, subtle, approval through her silence.

Danny returned home from college with a surprise: a bride. After the shock of his marriage wore off, his choice of a wife wasn't very surprising. That he "took" Ann, a pretty, stately, classy, yet aloof woman for his wife, was predictable.

His parents, particularly his father, were pleased. They felt Ann was just the influence needed to settle him down. As if on schedule, Ann designed a beautiful home which they built on a piece of Dad's property, and they had the requisite two children. Danny, of course, went into and later took over his father's business.

Throughout the years Ann remained a classy yet aloof attachment on Danny's arm. In many ways her personality was like that of her father-in-law. Danny continued being the dutiful husband and father but the sparkle in his eyes had dimmed.

In 1978, POW! They separated and the twinkle in his eyes returned. At this point in his life, Danny was a mature, successful businessman who oozed sex appeal. As in his younger days he drank, only this time it was scotch instead of beer, and he made love in luxury hotel suites rather than the back seat of cars. One thing remained the same: his choice of playmates. All were earthy and fun loving.

Ann continued her pretentious, withdrawn existence. She denied any knowledge of Danny's wild life style and stoically sat in her beautiful house waiting and waiting. The town gossips uttered the same unrelenting comments, "Poor Ann, how could she LET him do this to her? . . . We always knew he wouldn't grow up."

A closer look suggested Ann had other options. She was attractive, creative, and on solid financial footing. Her stoicism was part of her *Poor Me* game. So long as she retained herself in this position, she maintained her image and was seen as the innocent victim of Danny's irresponsibility.

What about Danny? For the past 12 years he had shifted responsibility for his lack of fun onto Ann. Marrying a woman much like his father, who kept him in check with nose to the grindstone, set up a game of *If It Weren't For You.*[1] Blaming Ann for his plight enabled him to convince himself that if it weren't for her, he'd have more fun. This rationalization permitted him to shirk responsibility for his own feelings and behavior, and, for the present, leave her.

How did this come about and how will it end? Let's start with the dynamics of their marriage. Danny was a bright, happy-go-lucky guy who valued fun and financial success. His father taught him how to make money and his mother showed him how to have fun with it. To have both fun and financial success, he needed a strong, unemotional woman who could provide him with structure and limits. These were the holes she filled for him.

Danny's behavior and feelings toward Ann were similar to what he experienced as a youngster with his father. With both, he played *If It Weren't For You.*

Ann keeps herself locked into the situation with games centering around money, security and her *Poor Me.* She came from an upper middle-income family, and had learned to value money and possessions as a way to feel secure. In her family, security was measured in terms of dollars and cents. Since security was associated with marriage, divorce was not an acceptable option. She also believed divorce would lower her from her pedestal down to the level of the common folk. Since her capacity for spontaneity, warmth and fun was limited, by attaching herself to Danny, she could vicariously taste this part of life. These were the holes he filled for her.

Since neither is a fully functioning, independent person in his own right, their attraction and marriage were based on their perceptions and unconscious beliefs about what the

[1]Eric Berne, M.D., *Games People Play,* Grove Press, Inc., New York, First Ed. Paperback, 1967, pgs. 50-58.

other could provide. For these reasons, Ann sits home while Danny plays and neither has filed for divorce.

Each is only half a person, needing the qualities the other can provide. The probability is that they will reconcile, only to reenact this very same scene at a later point.

Without significant change in their personalities, whether they divorce or not is irrelevant; they will continue to shift responsibility for their feelings and behaviors onto each other. If they divorce, they will continue playing their marital games into and through the divorce, until they find another suitable player. Should they remarry, it is a safe bet the new spouse will have many of the same characteristics as the original.

What kind of after divorce games will Danny and Ann play? *Games Divorced People Play* is about all the Dannys and Anns, Bobs and Susans, Toms and Cindys. Our focus is not creative divorce or the courage to divorce; rather, it's on what's for real, how you got there, and how to stop.

—**Melvyn A. Berke**
—**Joanne B. Grant**

SEMANTICS

We have used the pronoun "he" without sexual prejudice and for the purposes of grammatical simplicity. In reference to the custody parent, we have used the pronoun "she" because the majority of custody parents are mothers. The case histories have been drawn from our professional experiences. Some are composites, and all have been masked from outside recognition.

CONTENTS

1

WHO CHANGED THE RULES IN THE 8TH INNING?

The *divorce is final.* You have just joined the fastest growing minority in America. If our numbers continue to grow at
their current rate, we may become the pained majority. Imagine the potential effects — books, newspaper columns,
magazine articles and T.V. talk shows dealing with the problems of the oppressed married minority.

Despite the rampant rate of divorce, marriage is here to
stay. In view of the numbers of divorced people who remarry,
it is a safe conclusion that the divorced, for the most part, are
solid supporters of the institution of marriage. One thing
seems certain—the direction of marriage is changing. A new
consciousness stimulated by a flood of books, the Women's
Movement, and men's new choices have pried people away
from traditional roles, standards and ways of thinking.

The original concept upon which marriage was based
was grounded in personal and economic security. Love and
romance played little part in the selection of a mate.
Throughout history matchmaking was an honorable profes-
sion. In a good match the man took care of his family through
the fruits of his labors in return for a woman's nurturing,
children and sex. The arrangement was efficient and well-
defined.

John, his father, grandfather, and great grandfather knew exactly what to do to run *their* families. Their wives could look back at mother and grandmother and use them as role models. These firm, traditional roles and standards of behavior left little room for uncertainty, doubt or change.

The rapid advancement in technology spurred by World War I sparked the beginning of the end for traditional marriage. Prior to 1900 everyone knew where a woman's place was. During the Teens the pushy, blasphemous Suffragettes bandied their banners and tossed their bloomers aside. Rosie the Riveter and her compadres took to the assembly lines during World War II performing heretofore men's work.

The Fifties were ushered in by Kinsey, Brigitte Bardot and *Playboy*. Bardot not only wore a bikini like it was meant to be worn, but acted like she enjoyed being looked at and touched. The message was loud and clear — women could enjoy sex, too!

The Sixties were a time of controlled chaos. Vietnam, acid rock, the flower children, campus riots and communes were the death rattle of traditional mores and standards of conduct.

The Seventies have been termed the "Me Generation." In search of individual freedom and liberty, many have focused exclusively on themselves. It is as if they were unaware that what they did and what they said affected others.

As a result of these changes in attitudes and behaviors, the traditionally married couple of the late Forties and Fifties woke up one morning to find that someone had changed the rules in the 8th inning. Their firmly defined roles and expectations had evaporated. Housewife became a demeaning term to many. Being the man of the family no longer meant, "I'm the boss." The question became, "How do we play the 9th?"

While personal and economic security remain vital reasons for legal marriage, even they have taken on a different complexion. The easement of economic, occupational and credit discrimination against women has given them greater freedom and less reason to be dependent on men. This has also taken a burdensome and restrictive load off many men.

In the past, John did X, Mary did Y; they had children and remained together no matter what. As they worked for the common good, the family, their lives may never have touched, except perhaps momentarily. Intimacy was hardly an issue. Now people are becoming more aware of their needs and wants for intimate contact with other caring human beings. While the "Do My Own Thing" and "Intimacy" attitudes may seem divergent and conflictual, they are, in fact, complementary. Their interdependence grows out of the fact that genuine intimacy (warmth, honesty and sharing) can only develop from an attitude of personal responsibility.

Through our workshops, the consultation office and mail, we have learned that many divorces are the result of failure to comprehend and integrate these attitudes into a consistent and meaningful philosophy. As people involve themselves in a growth movement, at first, they often develop a "Screw you, it's your problem" attitude. This misinterpretation of the concept of individuality reflects a misunderstanding of power, aggression and assertiveness.

The "It's your problem" philosophy is an attacking, aggressive position which doesn't allow for real listening and sharing of wants, needs and thoughts. While assertiveness is also a non-passive position, *it does* permit listening and encourages understanding.

Assertiveness is the ability to create and maintain the conditions you want. It is a process and not an end in itself. This kind of power permits choices without losing sight of others. A truly powerful person is personally secure and has the wherewithal to negotiate or leave a situation without feeling the need to press on regardless of the consequences to himself or others.

The misunderstandings of the concepts of personal growth, responsibility, and assertiveness have been direct contributors to the burgeoning rate of divorce. In many instances Mrs. Smith entered therapy or one of the growth movements in order to be fulfilled, misunderstood the concepts, believed she was OK and her husband was NOT OK, and divorced. Six months later she finds herself confused, unable to deal with new, let alone old problems, becomes bitter and resentful, yet misses her husband to whom she is still emotionally attached.

Whatever the reasons, and regardless of who leaves and who's left, when the marriage ends, each spouse passes through a predictable sequence of feelings. We term this sequence the *Unhooking Process*.

UNHOOKING

Unhooking is giving up an emotional and romantic attachment to a person as well as to a relationship. This is a difficult and often lengthy process, lasting from one to three years. However, the bulk of the work is accomplished within the first six to ten months following the separation.

Hooked refers to holding onto an attachment despite the fact that in the now, the relationship no longer meets the emotional needs of either party. Refusal or inability to unhook is the brick and mortar from which most "After Divorce" games are conceived, nurtured and thrive.

The difficulty in unhooking from a spouse is the product of what Dr. Robert S. Weiss termed the "Attachment Process."[1] Marital attachment takes approximately two years to develop and is the binding together with another that gives rise to feelings of safety, comfort and at homeness when the other is present, or felt to be accessible. These feelings persist even when both parties view the marriage as over.

Stages of Unhooking

1. Surprise — It is difficult to imagine many situations in which signposts of a floundering marriage are not present. Surprise suggests that the leaver may not have been honest or that the left may have been wearing psychological blinders.

2. Disbelief — This is reflected in such thoughts or statements as, "How can she/he do this to me? This can't be happening to me."

3. Hurt and Abandonment — These feelings originate in very early childhood and result from fears of parental

---

[1]Robert S. Weiss, *Marital Separation*, Basic Books, Inc., New York, 1975.

loss and abandonment. In the present they are related to the broken promises, breach of trust and the loss of a spouse.

4. Guilt and Embarrassment — Feelings of guilt are usually a result of the belief that we have done something wrong, or should have behaved differently. Self-blame can also be a form of self-protection. By blaming oneself the criticism of others may be robbed of some of its clout. Embarrassment is a social consequence of internalized guilt.

5. Anger — Anger is a powerful feeling, and withholding or denying it can be personally and interpersonally destructive. It matters little if your feelings are appropriate. What does matter is that you feel and express your anger in a safe, non-destructive manner. Defuse your anger by screaming, beating on a pillow or by some other form of strenuous physical activity.

6. Resentment — Resentment over almost any issue, significant or minuscule, can crop up at the most unexpected moments. Brooding over what you disliked, what you lost, or what you could or should have had only leads to increased pain, depression or anger.

7. Grief and Mourning — As we detach and let go of our old identity as Mr. Smith, a husband, or Mrs. Smith, a wife, we enter into a period of mourning. In death the loved one is gone and his or her absence is marked by a ceremony, the funeral. In divorce, the loved one lives on, and usually with another.

8. Resolution — Resolution of bad feelings and emotional acceptance of the divorce is the final stage. Until you emotionally accept the divorce — unhook — you are as vulnerable as an open wound.

   You are unhooked when you can see, hear or interact with your ex without feeling bad. You are unhooked when you can perceive your ex as different and distinct from you.

2

"T.A. ETC."

We'd like to take you on a short and important side trip which will give us a common language and help you understand "After Divorce" games. Our brief excursion is into the ideas and language of Transactional Analysis, better known as T.A. T.A. was spawned out of the genius of a practicing psychoanalyst, the late Dr. Eric Berne. The success and popularity of T.A. is due to two factors—it works and it is understandable.

As with progress in any area, the "new crop" of T.A. theoreticians are slowly but surely improving and refining the original product. Refinement means one thing to the trained therapist, but another to the layperson. The more it's refined, like grains of sugar, the harder it becomes for people to grasp, understand and apply to everyday life.

In this chapter we introduce some of the basic concepts of T.A. In later chapters we explain "After Divorce Games" in a way you won't have to pay a professional to explain it to you.

EGO STATES

The concept of Ego States is the basis upon which Berne developed T.A. The three ego states — Parent, Adult and Child — and their subparts — Critical Parent, Nurturing

Parent, Little Professor, Free Child and Adapted Child — are ideas, notions and concepts we carry around in our heads. They are not real people! The ego states comprise the human personality and in a normal person are fairly well-developed by the age of eight. When we refer to an *ego state* (Parent-Adult-Child), it will be capitalized in order to distinguish it from a real person.

Adult

The Adult is that part of our personality that gathers information in order to analyze, compute and solve problems. Like computers, the Adult is devoid of emotions. Its job is to gather and store information to solve problems.

The efficiency of our Adult is affected by our physical health, our native intelligence and the degree to which it has been temporarily or permanently impaired by brain injury, drugs, alcohol or intense feelings, which contaminate its ability to function.

Parent

The Parent is the set of beliefs, messages and information that we received as children from our adult caretakers, and never bothered to check out and update in the here and now. While many parental messages are useful in adult life and had survival value when we were children, in the present some may be harmful. Parental messages are like taped voices in our heads that tell us what and how we should think, feel, and behave.

Berne identified two parts of the Parent, the Prejudiced or Critical Parent and the Nurturing Parent.

Critical Parent

The Critical Parent is filled with opinions and judgments about most everything — from how to dress, to politics, to the proper way of eating spaghetti. These opinions are often irrational because they are carried forward into the present, believed and acted upon without first being processed through the Adult. It is through the Adult that opinions, judgments and beliefs are validated to see if they are relevant to today's realities. Once this occurs the belief becomes a value or ethic. Without this process a belief or judgment remains prejudiced because its acceptance is based on another time, place and person.

Typical Critical Parent words are "never," "ever," "should," and "always." The Parent tapes in our heads, much like the words of our real fathers and mothers, are editorial and judgmental, e.g., "ridiculous," "childish," "wicked," and "immature." A loud brash voice, furrowed brow, finger pointing or hands on hips are non-verbal cues that the Critical Parent is out and in charge.

Nurturing Parent

When a child has been nurtured and properly cared for by his parents he grows up with the capacity to give and nurture himself and others. If he received proper care and protection, not overprotection and infantalizing, he will have learned and become capable of setting appropriate limits for his own children. These children, in turn, will grow up with the capacity to behave in a warm, caring manner toward other adults, and won't withhold their real feelings or be embarrassed when given to or cared for by others.

Child

Everybody has a little boy or girl inside him or her. This is the child he or she once was. There are three subparts of the Child Ego state: the Natural or Free Child, the Little Professor and the Adapted Child.

Free Child

The Free Child is the very young, impulsive, expressive part of the personality that wants what he wants when he wants it! He seeks pleasure over pain, is unashamedly sensuous, curious, and without an inner censor or authority that says NO!

As the little person grows and develops, he must learn to alter or delay some of his impulsive Free Child wants. While some degree of adaptation to the world is necessary, our Cultural Critical Parent has been so restrictive that many people lose or bury the freedom and vitality of their Free Child. These kinds of people are usually thought of as overly controlled, rigid, and distant.

It is vital that people maintain the ability to express their Free Child in adulthood. It is this capacity that adds the dimensions of warmth, charm, and sensitivity to the personality. Adults who maintain this capacity are usually described as warm, spontaneous, sensual and fun to be around.

The Free Child is not all fun and happy-go-lucky. All feelings reside in this part of the personality. Fear, anger, aggression, jealousy, etc., are also present and capable of being expressed. When these impulses are openly acted upon, without regard to others, harm is likely to result. Therefore, it is important that the Adult be the executor of the personality giving the Free Child permission, at the right time and place, to express itself.

Little Professor

The creative, intuitive part of the Child is called the Little Professor (L.P.). Despite its powers of intuition and ability to reach creative solutions, because it resides in the Child it is not well-informed and oftentimes reaches incorrect conclusions. Notwithstanding its vulnerability to errors, the L.P. is creative because it acts without fear of stepping outside the boundaries and limits set by others. Used in concert with updated Adult information, the L.P. can be a powerful ally. Most creative people, be they scientists, writers, artists or chefs have this one common denominator — a well-developed L.P.

Adapted Child

The Adapted Child (A.C.) is a modification of the impulsive, "I want it now" Free Child. Adaptations and delay of immediate gratification develop in response to the demands of authority figures in the little person's life. The developing child adapts out of his will to survive, his need for approval, and such basic emotions as anxiety and fear.

Many of our adaptations are appropriate when acquired in the interest of social custom and personal hygiene — e.g., toileting. However, most of us become overly adapted and as a result, quite early in life, begin to lose or deny what we really feel, think and want.

Appropriately adapted children learn to be aware of

others, to share, to be sociable and caring. They learn the skills necessary to help them relate without sacrificing their own social and interpersonal wants and needs. The overly adapted child lives in a state of NOT OKness, thinking and behaving according to what his parents want, or he thinks they want (Parent tapes). The always cautious, calm, overly compliant nice guy who avoids confrontations at all costs lives in his NOT OK Adapted Child. Dr. Muriel James and Dorothy Jongeward believe that the Child ego state is the foundation upon which a person's self-image and feelings of OKness and NOT OKness rest.[1]

All three ego states, and their subparts, are vital for a fully functioning, vibrant life. Now that we have some understanding of the structure of the personality, let's take a look at how it works.

If we draw three circles, each representing one of the ego states, John Jones would look like this (Figure 2-1):

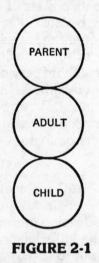

FIGURE 2-1

If we take into consideration the subparts of the various Ego states, John becomes a little more complicated (Figure 2-2).

---

[1]Muriel James and Dorothy Jongeward, *Born to Win*, Addison-Wesley Publishing Co., 1971, pg. 137.

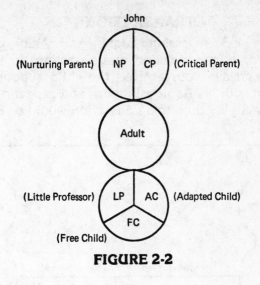

FIGURE 2-2

Since people interact with other people, let's draw our three circles or people side by side (Figure 2-3).

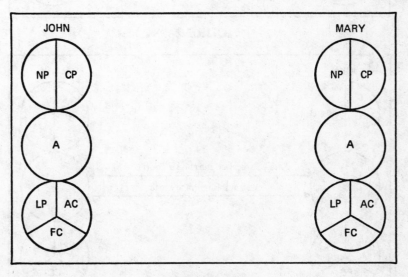

FIGURE 2-3

TRANSACTIONS

Figure 2-3 represents John and Mary potentially available for communication or transacting. In Figure 2-4 John asks, "Have you received the child support check?" Since John is in his Adult asking for and expecting information from Mary's Adult, this transaction would be diagramed as follows:

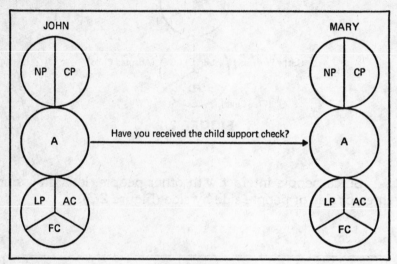

FIGURE 2-4

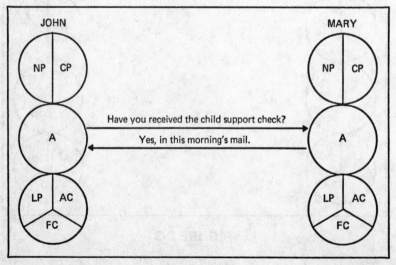

FIGURE 2-5

If Mary answers with the correct and expected response (Adult to Adult) the diagram would look like this (Figure 2-5).

This kind of transaction is called a parallel transaction because John spoke to, expected and received a reply from the ego state he addressed, Mary's Adult. Parallel transactions can occur between any ego states (Figures 2-6 and 2-7).

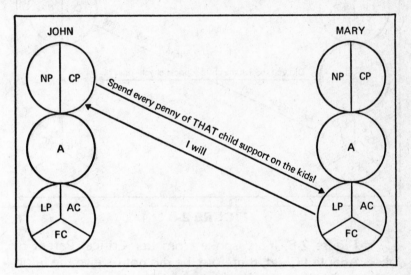

FIGURE 2-6

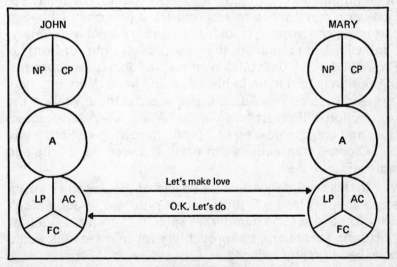

FIGURE 2-7

If, as in Figure 2-8, John asks Mary, "Did you receive the child support check?" (Adult to Adult) and she replies from another ego state, the chances for conflict are high.

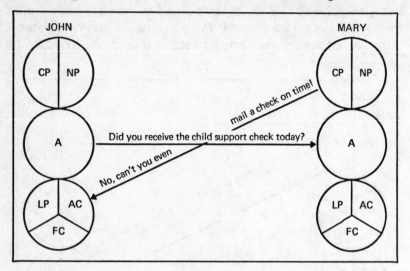

FIGURE 2-8

In Figure 2-8, Mary spoke from her Critical Parent to John's Adapted Child; therefore, he did not receive the information or type of reply he expected. The transaction or lines of communication crossed. At this point John has many options and can choose to respond from any one of his ego states. He can respond from his Nurturing Parent with, "Mary, I know it's been tough but things will be all right" or from his Free Child with, "Quit bitchin', it's sent!" John's most promising option is to remain in his Adult and invite Mary into hers by re-addressing her Adult. If she accepts the invitation the transaction will revert to a parallel Adult ◄─► Adult transaction, and communication and problem solving can proceed.

Crossed transactions can occur between any of the ego states (Figure 2-9).

In this case Mary asked for physical intimacy and love. Instead she received a Critical Parent putdown. If John didn't want to have sex, he could have said "no" from his Adult or Nurturing Parent and the probability for hurt feelings would have been greatly reduced.

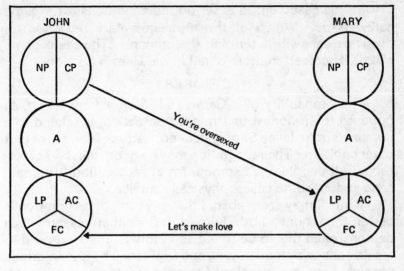

FIGURE 2-9

The Ulterior transaction, which always occurs in games, is the last one we will discuss. It is called Ulterior because it says one thing but means another. Hidden beneath the surface is a second or ulterior meaning (Figure 2-10).

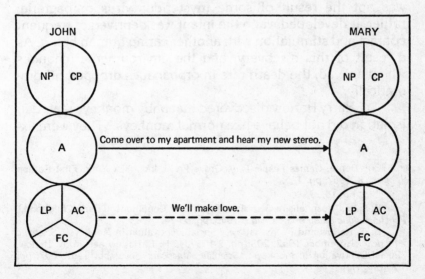

FIGURE 2-10

In this case John has set up the conditions for a game called *Rapo*.[2] Which of the messages Mary responds to, music or sex, will determine the outcome. The Rapo game will be discussed in more detail in the Games Section.

STROKES

The probability of a Game and Ulterior transaction, as opposed to an honest or straight transaction, is related to a person's stroke level. Simply defined, a stroke is an act or unit of recognition.[3] The recognition may be good, fair, bad or tortuous. All people need some form of recognition to remain sane and, in some cases, physically survive.

While it may seem absurd that any form of recognition is better than none, both human and animal research has demonstrated this to be true. Laboratory animals exposed to electric shock or loud noises, and frightened by non-injurious physical handling, developed more rapidly and were bigger, heavier, and stronger than those reared in isolation.

In the first quarter of this century, Dr. Rene Spitz described a syndrome termed "Marasmus" or "Anaclitic Depression."[4] This condition caused the deaths of thousands of infants who were being reared in extremely hygienic group homes and orphanages. Dr. Spitz discovered that Marasmus was not the result of some mysterious virus or bacteria; rather, it developed when the infant was deprived of frequent contact and stimulation with another caring human being. As a result of this discovery, and the environmental changes which ensued, the death rate in orphanages dropped off dramatically.

Dr. Harry Harlow discovered that baby monkeys reared in isolation did not behave like normal monkeys.[5] They were ex-

---

[2]Eric Berne, *Games People Play*, Grove Press, Inc., New York, First Edition Paperpack, 1967, pg. 125.

[3]Ibid., pg. 15.

[4]R. Spitz, "Hospitalism: Genesis of Psychiatric Conditions in Early Childhood," *Psychoanalytic Study of the Child I*: 1945, pg. 53-74.

[5]H. F. Harlow and M. K. Harlow, "Social Deprivation in Monkeys," *Scientific American*, November 1962, 203: pg. 2-10. Also H. F. Harlow and M. K. Harlow, "Social Deprivation in Monkeys," *Scientific American*, November 1962, 207: pg. 136-146.

tremely fearful, did not know how to play, be a part of monkey society or have sex. Left on their own, they remained huddled in a corner, withdrawn and isolated. In many ways they resembled severely emotionally disturbed human beings.

One of the most dreaded forms of punishment is solitary confinement. Not only have the Armed Forces studied this condition, they have also trained soldiers to withstand lengthy periods of isolation without cracking. The stories of the crew of the *Pueblo* detained in solitary confinement in North Korean prison camps are excellent examples. As a result of their training, these men devised methods of communicating in order to keep active and interested, to avoid withdrawing into a world of fantasy from which some may never have returned.

Laboratory studies of sensory deprivation are additional evidence of man's need for stimulation and stroking. Subjects deprived of external stimulation rapidly became intensely anxious or panicky, and some experienced hallucinations. In the more dramatic of these studies, subjects were suspended in water and bundled in such a manner that little or no external stimuli reached their senses. For more than very brief periods this is an intolerable condition.

There are four basic kinds of strokes: (1) Positive (2) Negative (3) Conditional and (4) Unconditional.[6]

A Positive Stroke is a positive unit of recognition, i.e., a compliment, gift, hug, smile, etc. A Negative Stroke is a negative unit of recognition, i.e., a putdown, scowl, physical abuse, etc. Conditional Strokes are based on certain conditions, i.e., a good report card, physical beauty, compliance, winning the race, etc. To obtain Conditional Strokes you must perform. Unconditional Strokes are freely given without regard to doing or not doing. Conditional and Unconditional Strokes can be either positive or negative. Figure 2-10 illustrates the possibilities.

---
[6]Muriel James and Dorothy Jongeward, *Born To Win*, Addison-Wesley Publishing Co., 1971, pg. 41-59.

The meaningfulness and intensity of strokes is variable. With each added bit of sensory input, strength and intensity increase. Compare the Unconditional Positive Stroke, "I love you," stated in a dull monotone, with "I love you," said with warmth, vibrancy, eye contact and a touch or hug.

Strokes are the social and physical lifeblood of the human condition. The kind of strokes we received and learned to expect in childhood are those we strive to *recreate* as adults. The child who was continuously stroked negatively for being clumsy will, in all likelihood, unconsciously create a life style in which he will be the inept bungler. While on the surface he may dislike these assaults on his OKness, at the deeper levels, he is receiving recognition the way he knows best. The same holds true for the child who was positively stroked for his curiosity and creativeness. Since these kinds of behaviors led to positive recognition and affirmed his OKness, this child will learn to value creativity, exploration and curiosity.

Rule of Thumb: What you stroke in others is what you get back in return. This is the basis for the statement that all behaviors serve a purpose. From the thousands upon thousands of strokes which impinge upon the infant, the little person develops his Life Script and concept of self. The script is nothing more than a design or plan for living. Most often it is beyond awareness. Psychological games are tools by which we obtain strokes in order to reinforce our life script. Through study or therapy people can become aware of their script, thereby changing the kinds of strokes they work for.

TIME STRUCTURING

Since "After Divorce Games" are one way people structure their time, a brief discussion of time structuring is in order. Berne lists six ways people can structure or organize their time.[7]

1. Withdrawal — A person can withdraw physically or even psychologically by moving into a world of fantasy.

---

[7]Eric Berne, *Games People Play*, Grove Press, Inc., New York, First Edition Paperback, 1967, pg. 36-48.

Withdrawal behavior can originate out of any of the three ego states.

An Adult decision to withdraw can be rational and based upon a desire to take personal stock of oneself, relax, or attend to some personal matter.

It may originate out of the Parent if it emulates that of the original parents; i.e., do you become furious and slam the front door behind you like Dad did every time your wife is about to confront you over your drinking?

Withdrawal emanating from the Child ego state is oftentimes a re-enactment of a person's childhood ways of protecting himself from pain, conflict, and frustration.

2. Rituals — Rituals are simple, stereotyped, complimentary transactions programmed by social events. Greetings, introductions and goodbyes are typical ritualistic behaviors. "Good Morning," "How are you?" or "How are you feeling today?" said as you pass an acquaintance or fellow worker in a corridor are not meaningful inquiries into their state of health or well-being. These kinds of transactions provide low intensity, positive, or maintenance strokes which grease the wheels of social conduct.

While rituals save time and promote social flow, they can be harmful if they are a person's only, or primary, way of relating.

3. Pastimes — Pastimes occur in social settings and vary in degree of complexity. Pastimes constitute the superfluous chit-chat which occurs at cocktail parties and social gatherings. Over and above their time structuring and maintenance stroke properties, they provide the possibility of getting to know others in a non-threatening casual setting. This type of transaction permits the Child portion of each person the opportunity of checking out the other in order to determine whether or not more in-depth contact is desired. Rituals and pastimes provide the basis for the selection of acquaintances which may lead to future friendships.

4. Activities — Activities are what people need, want and have to do. They range from jobs to household chores to stamp collecting.

When people give up or stop their usual activities, feelings of loneliness, emptiness, and restlessness often follow.

What happens when Mrs. Jones' children leave and Mr. Jones reaches the magic age of retirement? Unless these years are carefully planned and appropriate activities developed, physical and emotional deterioration is the rule rather than the exception.

5. Games — Berne defined a game as, "an ongoing series of complimentary ulterior transactions progressing to a well-defined predictable outcome."[8] He differentiated games from other modes of time structuring by their underhanded ulterior quality and the presence of a psychological payoff. As opposed to rituals and pastimes, most games are basically dishonest and have a dramatic as opposed to mildly exciting or stimulating ending.

A transaction or exchange between two or more people which contains the following elements is defined as a game.

1. A series of complimentary transactions which appear socially plausible.

2. A hidden or ulterior motive which is the *real* message.

3. A predictable feeling payoff which ends the game and signals the real purpose of playing.

   The formula for all games is:

   Con + Gimmick = Response ► Switch ► Payoff[9]

   Think of the Con as bait. It seems like one thing but really is another. The Gimmick is your playing partner's weakness or need. It is this player's weakness (Gimmick) which renders him or her vulnerable to the bait (Con). The reaction to the Con is the Response. The surprise ending is the Switch. The feelings the players are left with (usually bad) at game's end are their real reasons for playing—the Payoff.

Let's take a look at the game of *Rapo* described by Berne. Remember the Game Equation: C + G = R ► S ► P.

The Con (C) is the seductive attitude. The Gimmick (G) is the other player's desire for sex or power. If a woman initiates the game transaction, it is her Con that hooks into the Man's

---

[8]Ibid., pg. 48.

[9]Eric Berne, *What Do You Say After You Say Hello*, Grove Press, Inc., New York, pg. 23.

Gimmick. If he takes the Con and behaves amorously, the Response has occurred. If she then pulls the Switch with, "What kind of girl do you think I am?" a game transaction has occurred. The feeling state they leave with is their Payoff, or reason they played.

Games can be played at three different levels — first, second and third degree.[10] First degree Rapo is simple and open flirtation. The Payoff is usually good feelings and hope for a future encounter.

Second degree Rapo is better known as "Buzz Off Buster." In this instance the woman pulls the Switch by saying, "I'm not that kind of girl" (even though I led you to believe so). Her Payoff might be to gratify her feelings of resentment and spite toward men. The man might leave feeling rejected, put down or inadequate. If he is a frequent player, he may search out Rapo players to reinforce his belief that women are unreliable, no good tricksters.

While at the third degree intercourse may or may not occur, there is still a false cry of rape. The Switch is, "I'll call it rape anyway." In this instance her Payoff may be justification and spite, while his may be the fear and threat that she'll blow the whistle. Third degree players often end up in the morgue, hospital or court of law.

All games have a hidden psychological meaning and purpose. A female Rapo player may really be saying, "You're rotten like the rest of them." Her Payoff may not only be his discomfort, but also justification for her anger at all men. When her book of bad feeling stamps is filled she can, if she wishes, cash them in for her script Payoff, i.e., a free depression, suicide, addiction or prostitution. Her playing partner can also add another hurt to his book of hurts and, when filled, cash them in for his particular script Payoff.

These examples contain the primary elements of all psychological games and will help in understanding and appreciating After Divorce games. Don't be surprised if, at first, you yell foul, protesting your lack of participation. This is expected, because most games are played beneath one's level

---

[10]Eric Berne, *Games People Play*, Grove Press, Inc., New York, First Edition Paperback, 1967, pg. 64.

of conscious awareness. Only through self-study or therapy and a willingness to undefensively explore your behavior, feelings, and motives can you become aware of and alter your games. We suggest that those of you who yell the loudest, look the hardest!

6. Intimacy — Intimacy is free of hidden motives and exploitation. It occurs in those moments of human contact when feelings of closeness, tenderness, and affection have been aroused. Intimacy is genuine caring and closeness.

For many intimacy is risky because it leaves us open, available and vulnerable to another human being. We drop our screen and are exposed, naked, and unmasked for another to see and reach out to. Many avoid this risk preferring to structure their time around rituals, pastimes, activities and games. Recovering the capacity for and practicing the art of intimacy is the hallmark of a winner.

3

MONEY, MONEY, WHO'S GOT THE MONEY?

Games centered around money are probably the most frequent and hard fought negative transactions between ex-spouses. Not only do they affect the players themselves, they can also draw in children, friends, relatives and members of the business community.

Money games have little to do with the actual amount of money involved. The poor can play just as ferociously as the middle class and wealthy. Money enables us to get what we need and want. It is also a highly charged symbol that is used to reinforce our life scripts.

The fact is we need money. Without it life is a series of upstream struggles. When money is turned into a game transaction, it serves a psychological purpose. The game is not played for the sake of money alone. It is in this vein that we present some of the typical After Divorce Money Games.

If a couple played money games during their marriage, and most do, the chances are good that they will continue to do so through their separation and divorce. The seeds of all games, including After Divorce Games, are begun in childhood, develop and continue in the marriage, and are played during the separation and divorce. Despite discomfort, until a new player is found or the game is given up, the games continue because they are predictable and familiar.

The following letter written by a reader of our syndicated newspaper column "After Divorce" makes this point.

Dear Dr. Berke and Joanne Grant:

"I have had it with Women's Lib. My ex-wife wanted to be free, independent and responsible. Big Deal. She still keeps asking me for money and even tries to use the kids to blackmail me for money. I agreed to her terms at the time of the divorce, but it seems that wasn't enough. Does she think she can eat her cake and have it too?"

A: We find it less than coincidental that she "still" has to ask for money. Did she "have to" when you were married? It seems clear that both of you are still playing money games. Since you have a legal instrument for handling financial matters, but you continue to "get" each other over money, what's your reason for playing?

In order to stop gaming, and it takes two to play, ask yourself the following questions. Is the support adequate? Has it kept up with inflation? Have there been some realistic and significant changes in the children's lives that necessitate more money? Have you lived up to the letter and spirit of your divorce decree by sending, and on time, the full amount of support?

If you answer "no" to any of these questions, you are setting yourself up for continued negative interaction. Many couples arrange for such warfare in order to keep their relationship alive with transfusions of hostility.

After considering the facts make a clear cut statement to her about what she can and cannot count on from you. If she still asks for more put your anger aside because the next time around she will probably ask for the whole bakery.

In large part money games are based on cultural scripting. Most middle class men grew up with the Judeo-Christian work ethic, which dictated hard work, financial success and provision for their families. Middle class girls traditionally grew up to become housewives. They took care of their husbands, kids, and the house, and the men took care of the families' financial needs. They both operated out of similar belief systems. If the system is disrupted, as in divorce, yet their beliefs remain, they may continue behaving as if the system is still viable.

In many middle income families, the man is pro-grammed to be the provider, the woman a dependent nur-turer. It is easy for a woman to push a man's guilt and pro-vider button and for him to push her dependent nurturing button. Under these circumstances all the elements of a money game are present, particularly if emotional unhooking hasn't occurred.

Women with less education and lower income behave dif-ferently. While these women also hope to be taken care of when they are grown, they are more aware that they may have to take care of themselves. Their experience and perception has often shown men to be financially unreliable. Due to their limited education, their entry level into the job market is low, and many have to turn to social assistance programs for financial aid. For some, the Federal Government has become the "Big Daddy" Critical Parent upon whom they depend.

Men within this social class typically have well-developed Critical Parents. However, many are unsure about their ability to provide. After watching their fathers, friends, and other relatives experience difficulties with money, they are more ready to ask for outside help.

At the poverty level, young girls grow up expecting that they will have to take care of themselves. Most do so by becoming dependent on the welfare system. There is a strik-ing similarity between these people and the bureaucratic systems with which they have to deal and the traditional male chauvinistic marriage. The women and children are depen-dent. The system is in charge.

The wealthy operate much the same as the middle class. Despite their monied position and social status, many of these women are still quite dependent. The difference lies in the fact that if their ex-husband shirks his financial respon-sibilities they can pick up the phone and call "Big Daddy" — their attorney.

When we are playing money games, we believe that we are dealing with facts (numbers) and are behaving out of our Adult. This is the most deceptive aspect of money games and the primary reason they are so difficult to become aware of and to stop.

Sara is deeply involved in the Women's Movement. For

five years she has played the same tune with the same complaints leading to the same angry, resentful feelings, "I can't make as much money as my no good S.O.B. ex-husband who left me with three kids."

While this may be true, her attitude and behavior have prevented her from moving to a better place. The fact that she keeps herself overweight, unkempt and spends nearly 80% of her time complaining about "him" only reinforces her "Poor Me Victim" position, thereby preventing personal growth and happiness. Her constant complaining, without making any real changes, serves a hidden psychological purpose. As long as she maintains herself in a downtrodden, victimized position, she gets lots of "Poor Me" strokes from her fellow victims and has an excuse to keep complaining, while the situation remains unchanged. This behavior keeps her relationship with her ex-husband alive. By not giving up her bad feelings she maintains an emotional attachment to him. She has never taken responsibility for her present position. Her psychological Payoff is anger, resentment, and the proof she needs to reinforce her belief that men are no damn good.

Remember, money games don't have a thing to do with the amount of money involved. We all play, rich or poor. The intensity, time and psychological Payoff is one's own personal story (Life Script) as you will see in the following money games.

WHEN WE WERE MARRIED YOU WOULDN'T...

This game can be played single, double or multi-handed. The thesis of the game is that one of the parties, but only after the divorce, "does" or "buys" what the other asked for when they were married. The ulterior motive behind this game takes many forms. The two most common are "Wanting to get him or her BACK" or "Wanting to get back AT him or her."

Bill and Margo divorced after 10 years of marriage. Bill, a successful businessman, handled the money during their marriage and was the final authority over any large purchases, just as his father had been. Like her mother, Margo was a good housewife and homemaker and by default agreed to let Bill handle the family's financial affairs.

One of their main sources of conflict occurred when Margo wanted to buy something Bill didn't. Their negative transactions over money often went on for weeks at a time. During this period Margo remained in her whining, pleading Adapted Child. Bill had a well-developed and practiced Critical Parent and in time would end the matter with a firm, parental, "No, and I won't discuss it anymore!"

Over the years and from her Victim Child position, Margo saved books and books of angry, resentful, bad feeling stamps, which she cashed in for a guilt-free, self-righteous divorce. Bill also collected his quota of bad feeling stamps, which he later cashed in by buying the very things Margo had always wanted. The game was usually initiated by a phone call from Bill.

> Bill: "Remember that dining room set you liked and we talked about buying? Well, I bought one just like it. How about coming over to see it?"
> Margo (Remembering how much she had wanted that set, their arguments over it, and Bill's anger over her outlandish expensive taste, she replied from her saccharine sweet Adapted Child): "That's nice."
> Bill (Hearing her lack of enthusiasm): "Well, I thought you would be more excited for me!"
> Margo: "I don't feel too well today. I've got to go."
> She hangs up and feels like vomiting.

With each new report, he cashed in another book and she added more stamps to her collection. Because she remained in her Adapted Child and the transactions were familiar, she stayed in the game. She continued collecting bad feelings while discounting herself with thoughts like, "I'll never be able to buy that myself," and "Maybe I really need him." She felt sad and resentful that he now used money for pleasure and luxuries, whereas when they were married he always kept his umbrella ready for that inevitable rainy day.

Bill refused to see that he was cashing in his anger stamps with this behavior. The clue to his underlying motive was his frequent thought, "She's a fool; she shouldn't have left me. Look at what I could have done for her." Margo's unwillingness to give up her anger and update her relationship with Bill (they are no longer married) reinforced the game transaction. Both were unaware that the game kept them emotionally involved and unhappily shackled to each other.

There are other variants of "When We Were Married You Wouldn't . . ." One version uses the children as carrier pigeons. Randy buys that new quadraphonic sound system that Melissa, his ex, had wanted and gives the kids just the demonstration they need to fill Mom in on all the details.

Joanie, the dumpy, frazzled housewife, takes off that 20 extra pounds, learns the art of makeup and wears the right clothes to make herself look like an aware, up-to-date woman. She is now the desirable, energetic woman her husband wanted, rather than a befuddled housewife with three kids forever draped around her ankles. She showed him!

In one of our divorce workshops, Meg told us of all the arguments she and Stan had about his refusal to allow her to buy pictures for their home. When she met him at his apartment, "supposedly" to discuss some important matters concerning the children, she saw he had hung pictures in every possible nook and cranny. On seeing this, she refused the bait, sat down, laughed and asked, "Why don't you hang a few pictures from the ceiling?" She was never set up for another report.

These games can also be played single-handed. We recall one woman's stored-up scorn, tears and anger after learning that her ex-husband furnished his apartment with all new furniture. He was keeping his financial commitment to his children. He was also furnitureless. To buy new furniture seems reasonable. Would she have felt as bad had he bought old, ugly furniture?

All money transactions are not gamey. If you "buy" or "do" without an ulterior motive, without attempting to hurt the other, a game initiation has not been made. If the other party responds as though you have, stay in your Adult, don't take the Con, and a game will be avoided!

LOLLIPOP

This is a tantalizing, string-pulling game with elements of blackmail. When played to its conclusion, each person tells his tale of woe with righteous indignation to whoever will listen.

We encountered this game at a cocktail party, when Glenn, a 40-year-old, successful businessman and divorcé of one year, worked himself up into a near rage as he told how every time he finally gave in to what his ex had been begging for, she turned into a full-fledged bitch. He couldn't understand her ungratefulness, change in attitude, or that her behavior may have been related to his. Some careful listening and questioning brought the "Lollipop" game into vivid focus. The basic elements were control and blackmail.

As a boy Glenn was called "My Big Man" by Mom and Dad, so he worked and worked to live up to their expectations and please them. No matter how hard or how long he worked, it was never quite enough. He ended up feeling confused and inadequate. These circumstances set the pattern for his life—acting big and powerful while feeling small and ineffectual.

After 17 years of marriage, Kay, Glenn's ex-wife, wanted some extra goodies. She didn't ask directly or demand a definite yes or no. Instead, she behaved sweetly out of her NOT OK Adapted Child in order to "earn" her lollipop.

Glenn, acting out of his NOT OK Critical Parent, enjoying this period of respect and power Kay had permitted, kept the candy store open by giving her a possible future yes. In effect, he held the *lollipop* at arm's length just out of Kay's reach. His underlying message was, "Maybe I will, but only if you act the way I want." Herein lies the element of blackmail and control. When she behaved the way he wanted he gave her the lollipop.

Kay got her lollipop, then pulled the Switch by saying, "You S.O.B — not, "Thank you, Big Daddy," as Glenn had wanted. Glenn's Payoff was to feel confused and inadequate just as he had in his marriage and childhood.

Kay's scripting primed her for this game. As a child she had to sit sweetly on Daddy's lap and give him a hug or kiss to get her allowance or that extra privilege. Most of the strokes she received were conditional—having to be "sugar, spice, and everything nice." She received few positive strokes for being Kay the curious, intelligent child she really was.

As an adult she felt angry and resentul over having to behave sweetly to get what she wanted. Nevertheless, she had been programmed well and continued this pattern of behavior. After all, it worked and she liked all flavors of lollipops from money to mink.

In Glenn's head, he is still a little NOT OK boy, and in Kay's head she is still a little NOT OK sweet girl. In reality they are big people playing for big stakes. Lollipop has become their favorite game. Their divorce isn't about to cause them to give up those giant NOT OK strokes that keep their script alive.

Another way of thinking of the "Lollipop" game goes something like this. A puppy barks for a bone. His owner holds it up and makes him dance. After some powerful begging he gets the bone. He then bounds off carrying it onto his master's carpet and makes a mess. Who wins?

LOOK WHAT IT COSTS

The opening move of this game is to act helpless, inadequate or stupid about money matters. The Con, which is designed to set the hook, sounds like a statement of facts and problems which the initiator claims he or she can't deal with due to lack of knowledge or skill. The Gimmick is the playing partner's belief that he or she has some special powers, resources, or skills. The basic thesis is, "I'm a helpless Victim. You are the resourceful Rescuer."

Paul and Nancy have been divorced two years. Paul maintains a close relationship with his two children and has frequent contact with his ex-wife. When he comes by to pick up the children, Nancy initiates the game with the following statements: "Oh Paul, look at what it costs. The dryer went out last week. The dishwasher is on the blink and the store charges $20.00 *just* for a service call. After paying for the dryer, Mary's new cheerleader outfit, and the soccer fees, I just don't know what I'll do if I have to buy or fix another thing."

At the social level these may "seem" like simple statements of fact. They are not. There is much more behind them as they reflect a Child-Parent (Victim-Rescuer) series of transactions.

Suspect this game if:

1. These kinds of statements are repetitively made.
2. They come in series.
3. They are made as open ended statements rather than direct requests.
4. You feel a pull to do something out of a "have to."
5. The initiator has taken little responsibility to correct the situation.
6. You're left with a bad feeling.

Although a direct request for additional financial aid was not made, Nancy's underlying message was quite clear. "Give me more money . . . you still need to take care of me." If Paul feels guilty or neglectful and turns her words into a request for help, he has permitted her Con to hook into his Gimmick.

Assuming Paul pays adequate child support and/or alimony, he could decline the game initiation by staying in his Adult or avoiding situations in which he will hear these kinds of statements. Remember, Paul has made himself available to listen to Nancy. If he responds by taking responsibility, not only does he reinforce her powerless position, but sets himself up for more requests. When she brings up another problem he may feel taken advantage of and retaliate with, "I'm sick and tired of having to pay to fix your problems!" With that she may *innocently* reply, "But Paul, I never asked you for anything." Paul will probably leave feeling confused, bewildered, and set up for the next Con.

RAGGEDY ANN AND ANDY

This game draws the children in as pawns rather than active participants. The children are used as objects of blackmail by inviting fathers to feel guilty or embarrassed in order to get more money.

This tactic also invites a mother deeper into NOT OKness as it reinforces her feelings of helplessness, inadequacy and irresponsibility. While on the one hand she maneuvers others to get what she wants, on the other, her behavior is but a reminder of her inability to act independently.

One move is for Mrs. Ex to send Ann and Andy over to visit Grandma and Grandpa (Daddy's parents) in their finest tatters. Ann is a bit raggedy, but neat and clean. Andy's pants, shirt, shoes and underwear are not only worse for wear but too tight. Judging from their neat appearance, it is apparent that Mrs. Ex is doing the best she can with what little she has. What grandparent would stand for this? It's a good bet that they will either admonish their son or do the rescuing themselves.

In this case Mrs. Ex's Con goes something like this: "I can't do it myself, so I'll get you to do it." Assuming adequate child support and/or alimony, any guilt, anger or embarrassment Mr. Ex feels or extra money he coughs up is generated out of his Gimmick, which says that he is the more powerful, potent, and responsible parent.

If he permits her Con to hook into his Gimmick and responds, he is setting himself up for more conning and is ripe for future pickings. If he has been financially responsible he can put his anger away, inform everyone of the financial commitments he has made and let Mrs. Ex deal with the situation.

If he takes the latter course, he's cut the game off at the point of initiation. No Gimmick-No Response-No Payoff. If he does this Mrs. Ex can also come out a winner. She will have the opportunity of learning how to be responsible with money, as well as how to ask honestly in legitimate times of need. If she plays harder and really lets the kids suffer, this game can escalate to the third degree level—the hospital or courtroom.

NO GROCERIES

"No Groceries" is a variant of "Raggedy Ann and Andy." Mrs. Ex initiates the game by continuously telling the children, directly or subtly, "All's poor on the money front." Her "No's" about money can range from that extra $15 for the "KISS" concert to, "I'm sorry we just can't afford to buy another head of lettuce this week."

Rest assured the kids will somehow manage to tell Dad. Mixed in with their words will be feelings of anger, rejection and possibly even abandonment for his letting them and their mother down. A transaction shared by a client went like this:

> Jan invited Allen, her "boyfriend," and his children, Bill and Barbara, over for dinner. Jan served fresh fruit salad with dinner and offered Barbara some, only to hear, "Yes, thank you. My mother won't buy oranges anymore. She says they are too expensive." Allen swiftly replied, "What do you mean you can't have oranges at home?" Barbara, sensing the sparks, softly replied, "Gee Dad, Mom just said we had to cut down."

The transaction ended with Dad stewing in his juices about how the child support was being spent and Jan valiantly trying to smooth ruffled feathers by offering empty reassurances.

Allen and his ex-wife had maneuvered themselves into this position and were equally responsible. Allen's ex-wife was still extremely angry, yet emotionally attached to him. She was, though unconsciously, using the children to show him up as the bad guy while attempting to appear guilt free. She was also trying to manipulate him into sending more money than originally agreed upon.

Although Allen was sending adequate child support, he was in an excellent financial position and their standards of living were vastly different. While not required by law, he could easily afford to increase the child support without adversely affecting his own standard of living.

That he reported this story at every opportunity indicated that he was also attempting to set her up as the villain. Dollars weren't the vital issue. They were still emotionally attached, though legally divorced, with each trying to control and show up the other.

YOUR POTENTIAL IS GREATER

This ex-to-ex game is usually initiated by the wife during the separation as a mechanism to gain that extra bit of leverage as they negotiate a property settlement. As with most other games, it may continue after a legal divorce.

The statement, "Your potential is greater," in and of itself doesn't necessarily signal a game initiation. Typically, a man's earning potential is greater than a woman's. The probability of a game developing depends on how, why and when it is said. When it is used as a Con to invoke guilt and manipulate to get more, it is a game initiation.

Joan and Bob's situation is a classic example. Joan filed for the divorce. She no longer loved Bob "romantically," felt that she was losing her identity, and that being married impeded her personal growth and development. Bob didn't want the divorce, but after numerous talks with Joan he gave up the ship.

As they worked toward the settlement, Joan pressed for more and more. Since Bob felt like a failure as a husband and wasn't thinking clearly, all she had to do was keep telling him that his earning potential was greater. It was like taking candy from a baby. During the negotiations she went about her merry way recarpeting, draping and refurnishing. The guilt-ridden Victim position Bob had adopted prevented him from doing anything other than looking on like a child as he paid the bills along with the alimony and child support.

Joan's Con was, "Your potential is greater." Bob's Gimmick was, "You're right, I'll pay for it." After getting what she wants Joan pulls the Switch with, "I got what I wanted so buzz off for *now*." She leaves feeling triumphant. Bob leaves the game feeling put-down, angry, and rejected.

I'LL ALWAYS TAKE CARE OF YOU

This game most often occurs among middle to upper income couples, is initiated during the separation, and continues through the early stages of the divorce. It is born and bred out of the chauvinistic belief and attitude that a man's OKness depends on how well he "takes care of his woman." A woman throws in her hand with the belief that her OKness rests upon how well he takes care of her.

During the early stages of separation, both are frightened, anxious and insecure. Traditional societal mores are supportive of women who openly express their feelings and look down upon, or at least aside at, men who show their feelings. This results in men witholding feelings while pledging eternal support and protection for their stricken mates.

A man's cultural scripting supports the fantasy, "I'll be there even when I'm gone." The female counterpart of this fantasy is, "I expect you to!" His Con is, "I'll always take care of you," with the ulterior message being, "I'll show everyone what a good man I am." Her Gimmick is "I need you to." Since the promise was made in a time of pain, hurt and irrationality, he can pull the Switch by saying, "I meant it when I said it, but it is just not possible." A harder "get back at" version is "You idiot, you really didn't expect me to support you for the rest of your life!" His Payoff is vindication, anger and superiority. Her Payoff is to feel rejected, inadequate, and angry.

A woman can also initiate the game with the Con, "I need you to take care of me." Her ulterior message here is, "I'll play at being weak and dependent to get what I want." His Gimmick is, "I'll show the world what a good moral man I am." She can then pull the Switch by finding someone else to take even better care of her and tell him to "Buzz Off." Her Payoff is a revengeful, "I got you." His Payoff is to feel inadequate, ineffectual and depressed.

This game can be avoided by not making or believing these kinds of almost impossible irrational promises that leave both tied to each other and primed for future hurts and games. Couples get caught up in this game out of their unwillingness to believe that *what once was, is no longer.*

I GOT SCREWED IN THE SETTLEMENT

Regardless of the fact that the same two people lived, hurt and grieved through the same divorce, if you spoke to them separately, you might never guess that they were talking about the same divorce, let alone each other. Seldom do two people, even eye witnesses, report the same event in the same way. Parties in a divorce settlement see things even more differently. Rarely have we heard both declare that they got a fair shake.

Most women in traditional marriages know little about their own financial affairs. Their first brush with the world of money will probably come about in the attorney's office. He'll ask numerous and important questions about financial matters for which they will have few answers. They may even be informed of the many devious ways some men have of hiding assets in order to "screw their wives." Confronted with these questions, a lack of information, the possibility of his deviousness, their first responses are likely to be fear, insecurity, and to wonder if he's "one of them."

As they stew over the situation and question their husbands, they may retaliate by becoming less communicative and uncooperative. This sets the stage for increased suspicion, distrust and unfounded allegations as to the other's motives and intentions.

Following the divorce and settlement, they may emerge from their cocoons of suspicion into an overt game transaction. The game may be played singly (only in one's head), two-handed or multi-handed by drawing in others. As with other games, the actual facts and circumstances matter little. The primary motives of this game are blame, self pity, inadequacy, anger and revenge.

The game begins by "It" telling anyone who will listen about the disastrous financial impact of the divorce. Played at the first degree level, "It" tells his tale of woe in order to get poor me strokes to justify his belief about how good he is and how bad she is. First degree players give this up quickly and go out after positive strokes to affirm their OKness. Second and third degree players are after revenge and use their poor me strokes to reaffirm their basic feelings of inadequacy, self-pity and NOT OKness.

Played single-handed, "It" plays and replays in his head all the things he or his ex did wrong, should have done differently or shouldn't have done. The bad feeling Payoff is defeat, inadequacy and depression.

In the two-handed version, each of the "Its" complains, puts down and accuses the other of taking advantage of him/her. These remarks can be openly aggressive, or take on more subtle manipulative forms.

"Bar Stool" is the multi-handed version of "I Got Screwed in The Settlement" with the Con being, "I tried to be fair and that S.O.B. took advantage of me." Matt's story is a prime example. Matt was fortunate to have friends who stuck by and supported him during the separation and early divorce crisis.

They often invited him to dinner and listened attentively as he offered such details as attorney's fees, the amount of his alimony and child support, what he had to give up, his troubles adjusting to a new lifestyle and how foolishly his ex-wife spent "his" money. In the beginning his friends were sympathetic and stroked poor Matt. After awhile they became bored, and the dinner invitations dwindled. Matt took some of his poor me to the office. He redoubled his efforts there to compensate for the loss of strokes from his friends. Gradually his co-workers also turned off and withdrew. As a result, his productivity decreased and his job was jeopardized.

With his friends and co-workers fleeing, he took his, "How could such a nice guy like me get the shaft?" for a drink. Every bartender and patron within earshot heard his sad story. When even these strangers turned away he became increasingly lonely, depressed and defeated. Six months later he was killed in a car accident, driving while intoxicated. Matt fulfilled his prophecy—Poor Matt.

Since settlements are difficult to change, a game which offers greater opportunity to get back AT is nonsupport.

NONSUPPORT

The notion that only low income, poorly educated men run out on the financial responsibility for their children is simply not true. Data indicates that a surprisingly large percentage of men in middle to upper income brackets are unreliable in meeting this responsibility. There are more than a handful of children whose fathers are doctors, lawyers, accountants, engineers, etc. who are on some form of social assistance or welfare program.

If a man purposely withholds support for any reason, he has initiated a game maneuver. The next move is up to his ex-wife. She may choose name-calling, whine out of the Victim position or take *immediate* and affirmative legal action. The latter course may cut the game off at the pass. The game may proceed up the ladder from first degree name-calling to third degree courtroom or jail.

Pete had been a successful systems analyst. He, Ruth and their four children lived very well, though beyond their means. Despite their custom built home, two luxury cars, and extensive traveling, they managed to stay ahead of the bill collectors.

Although Ruth disliked the situation, she enjoyed their standard of living and chose to bury her head in the sand, ignoring the facts of their impending financial plight. The greater their money problems, the deeper she buried her head; "After all, girls don't deal with money—that's man's work." To make matters worse, over the last several years of their marriage, Pete gave every indication of being both an unfaithful husband and a potential alcoholic. Ruth remained in her hole. When they divorced, the only asset she had left was that little hole in the ground.

By that time Pete was a dyed in the wool alcoholic. For awhile he was able to keep his job, but Ruth and the kids never saw a penny. As in her marriage, she pleaded with Pete from her Adapted Child. As usual Pete responded from his Critical Parent—the result was no money. After pleading, borrowing, and applying for food stamps, she finally looked to the courts for relief. The courts joined in and made the game three-handed. Like Ruth, they threatened, gave second and third chances, meted out brief, though ineffective, punishments, and in the end said, "Poor us — Poor Ruth . . . We have done all we can."

The judicial system worked like this. An officer of the court threatened Pete, "Pay or jail." Pete appeared in court six months behind in child support, looking like hell, and nearly broke. Aware that he can't work if he's in jail, the judge demanded he pay something now and the rest when able. He also extracted a promise from Pete to do better in the future. Naturally, Pete agreed. Of course, he did not do better. The scene was re-enacted over and over until he was several thousand dollars behind with absolutely no prospect, ability or intent of paying the back support.

The circle of threats, sporadic partial payments and promises continued. On three occasions he couldn't even come up with his usual pittance, so off he went to jail for 72 hours, then out again to restart the cycle.

Looking back over their situation, we can see that Ruth's

predicament was set up by her marital money games. Not only did she ignore and withdraw from the financial aspects of her marriage, she also ignored the many signposts of an impending divorce. She never took positive action to protect herself from financial disaster. Since she didn't prepare herself to enter the job market, when the time came she found herself without marketable skills and nearly destitute. Had she been realistic about Pete and given up her wish and fantasy that he would change and take care of her (I'll Always Take Care Of You), she would have made personal, financial, and occupational plans. Had she given up her myth about Pete, she would also have taken appropriate legal steps the very first time he missed a support payment.

Pete's Con was, "Give me a second chance." Ruth's Gimmick was, "Okay, I need you." Pete pulled the Switch by never paying. Ruth's Payoff was to feel victimized, helpless and indignant. Ruth arranged to be the victim in both her marriage and divorce to prove her childhood script decision, "Men are unreliable." Pete's life position was "I'm NOT OK — you're NOT OK." His Payoff was a childish titter and the thought, "I got you all." The tragedy was that in order to act out his life position he found it necessary to *get others* (You're NOT OK) and in the end *got himself* (I'm NOT OK).

———————————

Check out your memory bank! Get a pencil and paper and answer these questions.

1. As a child what did you observe about money?
2. How old were you when you first became aware of money—how to use it and abuse it?
3. In your parents' home, who was the breadwinner?
4. When you were a child, who made the major purchases?
5. If you asked to buy something, did Mom say, "We'll have to ask Dad?"
6. What were the disagreements over money?
7. How were the disagreements resolved?

8. What were your family's money habits? Were budgets, savings, credit and business openly discussed?

9. How did your parents look, act and talk when dealing with money matters?

10. What non-verbal messages did you pick up about money? Did one parent hide purchases from the other?

We all make unconscious decisions about our role in relationship to money. Look at your scripting regarding money. Most little girls were told that it wasn't important to learn about all those numbers . . . it just wasn't feminine. Little boys learned about numbers so they could grow up and become powerful "man" bankers, engineers, statesmen, C.P.A.s, architects, etc. In school, boys were supposed to be better at math and girls at English. Little boys even got to gamble with marbles. How many steelies or agates did a little girl win? Statistics was a common concept for boys through the world of baseball cards. Did you ever hear of any statistics on dolls? Boys' choices about money came under the heading of winning and losing, power and control. Girls' choices about money came under the heading of whom she married.

Update your Adult about money. Analyze your money habits and what money symbolizes to you. Adult can mean dollars and *sense*.

4

HAVE ORGASM WILL TRAVEL

In the weeks, months, or even years of deciding whether or not to remain in a marriage, at least one of the parties has created a world of divorce fantasy. These fantasies typically revolve around freedom, independence, the unknown, finances and the excitement of sex. For many, the grass seems greener in someone else's bed! The imaginings created during this period set the stage for disappointments as the world of reality comes crashing down.

During the separation and for a year or so after divorce, most people are obsessed with sex. The obsession may be in the form of sex as sport, or total abstinence.

The following letter from a reader of our newspaper column, "After Divorce," is not unusual:

> "I have fantasized all the wonderful good times and sexual turn-ons I would have as a divorced woman. I have had lots of dates and sex and it all adds up to a big nothing. I am depressed and care very little about men or sex. What's happened to me?"

This woman's disillusionment, anger and depression are based on the degree to which her pre-divorce fantasies did not match her after-divorce realities.

Why this drastic passing phase? As we studied After Divorce Sex Games, we came to recognize the following sequence through which most of the divorced pass.

Patty Cake

The Patty Cake period occurs after the initial shock wave and numbness pass and people can again look out on a world populated by sexual beings. At this point they are beginning to shake off the loss of their spouse and can feel their own juices and urges. During the Patty Cake period the recently divorced man or woman will do almost anything to be touched. They may become involved in sporting sex, prostitute themselves in order to lie next to a warm body, and temporarily abandon previous values and standards of conduct.

The single's bar is the main stomping ground of the Patty Cake player. The unattached congregate in their self-centered search for physical contact and sexual gratification. They crowd and mill about, touching, bumping and rubbing as they seek out tonight's pleasure partner . . .

> "Patty cake, Patty Cake
> Baker's Man
> Lay me, lay me
> You can, you can"

Terrible Two's

The Terrible Two's is the phase of frustration a person feels after running the Patty Cake gammit. You wake up, slap your hand, and realize you have been out playing while the rest of your life falls by the wayside. You become aware of your needs for the limits, structure and goals only you can provide.

Movin'On

In this stage people begin putting the pieces of their lives back together. Initially they complain, "Will I ever get it all together?" And yes, this is the time some will accomplish just that! Most will establish committed relationships. The latest data reveals that on the average, one out of two divorced persons remarries 3.1 years after divorce.[1]

---

[1]Population Reference Bureau, Inc., *Population Bulletin*, Vol 32, No. 5, February 1979. Updated Reprint, pg. 8.

Quadraplegic

Unless a person is Movin' On and is reconstructing his life, he may become immobile and need to be pushed, carried and prodded about because he feels inadequate or incapable. Alcoholism, drug abuse and sporting sex are *symptomatic* of the quadraplegic.

SEX AND STROKES

The primary reason for one night stands so often seen in the Patty Cake period is stroke deprivation. Sex is the simplest, most pleasant way of trying to satisfy and fulfill man's six basic hungers:[2]

* Contact Hunger
* Recognition Hunger
* Stroke Hunger
* Touch Hunger
* Taste Hunger
* Smell Hunger

Why, then, the emotional letdown and disillusionment with one night stands? The reason is stroke deprivation.

Think of a stroke deprived person as a battery in need of charging. The weaker the battery the greater the electrical charge needed to give it life. By the same token, the greater one's stroke deprivation, the more sexual activity one may engage in in an *attempt* to recharge the battery.

There are several problems with this tack. More often than not, the "screw 'em and leave 'em" scene is tedious work, requiring more effort than the return in emotional pleasure and positive strokes. People readily available for one night stands are stroke deprived themselves and, for the most part, are unable to give anything other than their bodies. They are like two run down batteries *trying* to recharge each other. The result is a shallow, transient interlude. Sex without caring or love can be physically satisfying and provide momentary release, but does little for the heart and soul.

---

[2]Eric Berne, *Sex In Human Loving*, Pocket Books, New York, 1971, pg. 184-185.

SEX AND LIFE POSITIONS

A person's view and evaluation of himself and the world about him is nearly developed by the age of eight. During these early years a youngster evaluates his experiences, decides on their meanings and the roles he is going to play in adulthood. Dr. Berne termed this process the child's "days of decision."[3] Since these decisions are made before the little person's Adult is fully developed, many are distorted and irrational. If they are not updated and are carried forward into adulthood, they can lead to significant problems.

These decisions form the basis of the four psychological positions described by Dr. Thomas Harris.[4]

Position 1: I'm OK, You're OK
A person holding this position has the capability to assess and realistically evaluate his life and circumstances and to effectively solve his problems. His expectations about himself and others are likely to be accurate.

Position 2: I'm OK, You're Not OK
People adhering to this life position feel persecuted and victimized and typically blame others for their problems. Delinquents and criminals often adopt this position.

Position 3: I'm Not OK, You're OK
Persons with this view continuously grade themselves and they always award themselves a failure. As a result they withdraw, become depressed and can become suicidal.

Position 4: I'm Not OK, You're Not OK
People with this position lose their zest and interest in life, withdraw, become depressed and are potentially homicidal or suicidal.

Psychological positions also become sexualized.[5] When forming one's identity a person often adopts a set of sexual

[3]Eric Berne, *Principles of Group Treatment,* Grove Press, Inc., New York, 1966.
[4]Thomas A. Harris, *I'm OK—You're OK,* Harper & Row, New York, 1967, pg. 37-53.
[5]Muriel James and Dorothy Jongeward, *Born to Win,* Addison-Wesley Publishing Co., 1971, pg. 35.

expectations and attitudes about himself and others which may be different from his other belief systems. This helps explain why some people feel good about themselves occupationally or socially and poorly about their ability as husbands, wives or lovers.

Sex can be an expression of intimate sharing and love, an act of aggression, a physical release, or a way to manipulate and control. The term or terms we use to refer to sex reflect our thoughts, feelings, and sexual life position. A not uncommon occurrence is to adopt the attitude that one sex is OK and the other not OK.

The same can be said about the purposes for which we use sex. There are a host of words, slang expressions and euphemisms which refer to sexual intercourse. Some of the more common are: roll in the hay, making love, fornication, screwing, coitus, a piece of tail, pussy, being intimate, a nooner, making a baby, affair, a quickie, a lay, one night stand, and nookie.

What terms would you expect a male to use who believes that men are OK and women are NOT OK? Conversely, what terms would he choose if he believes that both men and women are OK? What would you expect his reasons and purpose for having sex to be?

If couples with OK sexual life positions honestly evaluate and share their thoughts and feelings about the meaning of sex, most would agree that meaning varies with their personal and interpersonal feeling state. In an OK committed sexual relationship, each learns and understands what, for that moment, the sex act expresses. At times they are making love, at times screwing, and on occasion expressing domination and control, etc.

People who are indiscriminate in their sexual behavior or who take a Not OK position about the opposite sex tend to view sex along a narrow and negative dimension. The words and terms they use are *habitually* derisive and refer to only a portion of the anatomy, i.e., "boobs, pussy, rod, snatch, cock, dick and peter" rather than the total person.

Once a psychological position is adopted and integrated into the personality, behaviors are engaged in which reinforce and perpetuate these beliefs. It is out of one's life and sexual position, based on early experiences and decisions, that sex games are played.

SEX AND TAPES

Another factor which plays a significant role in our thoughts, attitudes and behaviors about life in general, and sex in particular, is our "Parent Tapes." A Parent Tape is a message (rule or belief) originally learned in childhood which is carried forward into adulthood without being updated in the here and now. For children these messages may have good survival value. However, they may be negative or restrictive to an adult. The tapes stored in our heads silently guide our behavior, and are replayed with increased and uncomfortable volume when we violate their messages. If as children we were taught that it is dangerous to go swimming soon after eating, and we do so, we may feel guilty or lessen our enjoyment for fear of cramping and drowning. To avoid the guilt or fear, we may act on the recording by waiting until the mandated time has passed. The same principle applies to sex tapes.

There are several ways to update a tape. The best is to gather data and evaluate it in the light of the now through our Adult ego state. If we disagree with the old information, we may eliminate it through a new Adult decision. If the updated information indicates that the old message is to our advantage, we can accept and incorporate it into our belief or value system. Another, though temporary and dangerous, way to reduce the force and stress of a taped message is to knock it out through the use of chemicals. Alcohol and drugs are common ways of accomplishing this. If you have an affair when you are drunk, it is an easy matter to shift responsibility for your behavior by blaming it on the booze; "I didn't know what I was doing—I was drunk."

While Parent tapes are based on old information, at the time they came into being most had positive value and fit with the times. For example, prohibitions about sex outside of marriage, prior to the development of reliable contraceptive methods, were quite appropriate. Today sanctions against sex based upon fear of an unwanted pregnancy are no longer viable.

As a fun learning experience, we often ask our After Divorce workshop participants to become aware of and share their sex tapes. The result is usually shock followed by a belly-laugh as they get in touch with the absurdity of some of their thoughts, feelings and behaviors which worked some 10-20 years ago, but may not fit with their present situation and circumstances.

Some of these sex tapes are:

Divorced women are ripe for screwing.
Marry a virgin.
Variety is the spice of life.
Have sex only in or after dark.
The more women you have the better man you are.
Women are the keepers of the morals.
Men are always ready, it's up to the woman to decide.
Nice girls don't do that.
Touching is inviting sex.
Living together is sinful.
Have sex only with your husband.
A single woman at a bar is asking for it.

Joni, a 40-year-old workshop participant, has been having sex with her ex-husband for five years. Despite their divorce and his remarriage, she feels perfectly comfortable with this arrangement. Since one of her powerfully programmed sex tapes was "only with your husband," she rationalized, "He was my only husband." With some work and a lot of support from the group, she was able to make a new decision to break with the past and seek new relationships. Her tape kept her locked into a go-nowhere relationship in which she felt guilty going out, let alone having sex, with a man other than her ex-husband.

In the Fall of 1977, we conducted the first workshop on divorce in Mexico in which we candidly dealt with such issues as separation, sex and living together. Since Mexico is a predominantly Catholic country and also has a strong machismo ethic, we were surprised when they openly and excitedly shared their thoughts and feelings about sex. When we introduced the notion of sex tapes, both men and women alike seemed delighted to get them out of the bedroom and into the open.

While somewhat different from ours, some of their tapes are:

Sex is only for prostitutes, not for your sister.

A man is like a dog . . . he can shake himself off and be clean again.

A woman must be loaded like a rifle . . . filled with child and in the corner ready to be used.

A woman shouldn't be touched even with a rose petal . . . she must be pure.

It takes only one bull for a herd of cows.

Talking about sex with a man is an invitation for sex.

Never do it after eating . . . the digestion is disrupted.

Tie up your hens because the cock is free — (take care of your daughters).

For the woman, not even all the love or all the money.

The Mexican Macho is like a brave bull . . . he has enough for all.

Are any of these sex tapes similar to yours? Is Mexico that different from the U.S.?

Remember, all games are transacted beneath our level of awareness. They are a way to structure time and to validate a particular belief or childhood decision. The surface behavior is also different from the true or ulterior motivation. Visualize the playing pieces, be they sex or money, as vehicles similar to the miniature toy used to hop around the Monopoly board. The real object is not the toy, sex or money, but rather landing on Boardwalk, going to jail or whatever will give you your psychological Payoff.

When Joe was a young child he received a lot of attention and strokes for his tantrums. By the time he was five his family had a host of stories they told about his outbursts. When Joe was married he had tantrums for which he received a lot of wifely attention. Joe is divorced and still has tantrums. What is more important: What he has the tantrum about, the tantrum itself, or the attention he receives as a result of his behavior?

Our discussion of After Divorce sex games will be divided into two sections: Wet and Dry games.[6] Berne defined a dry game as one which avoids confrontation with the naked body and therefore responsibility for defloration, impregnation, stimulation, affection and the other consequences of intercourse. A wet game ends in penetration and/or orgasm. Because they are games, intimacy is avoided and no commitment exists.

WET GAMES

HAVE ORGASM WILL TRAVEL

Jerry is a 28-year-old college graduate whose looks, charm and manner typify an Esquire magazine advertisement. He is successful, has a debonair manner, but has never established a lasting relationship. His only marriage endured all of three months. For the past year he has been the John Travolta of the swinging singles' set.

"Saturday Night Fever" Monday through Sunday is a tough grind. In search of positive strokes, Jerry has continued on this merry-go-round to the point of near exhaustion and depression. Although the Parent in his head tells him, "Here I go again," his stroke deprived Child trembles with anticipation and excitement over the possibility of "real love" rather than just another body. Part of him claims to want an intimate relationship. However, the singles' clubs he frequents and his choice of stroke depleted women assure him of only another ritualized sexual conquest.

Curiously, Jerry considers the singles' scene plastic, yet he reserves the head of the table for himself. Observing him is not an easily forgotten experience. Decked out in the proper disco attire, he struts with the requisite degree of macho, chooses the sexiest girl at the bar and begins his ritual. Although a superb dancer, his partner is little more than a beautiful bauble to aggrandize him. If a woman gets too close by making emotional contact, he distances and breaks the connection.

---

[6]Eric Berne, *Sex In Human Loving*, Pocket Books, New York, 1971, pg. 165-166.

As he "does his thing" he seems much like a bird going through its instinctual mating rite. He re-enacts this scene throughout the evening, leaving with the body most attracted by his charms. The night ends with the usual "slam bam thank you ma'm," along with the same nagging feeling of loneliness and disappointment.

The game transaction is this. The Free Child in him wants positive stroking and nurturing; nevertheless, his fearful Adapted Child prevents it. His Con is, "Let's have fun and sex." The ulterior message beneath the Con is to prove women are NOT OK. The chosen female, being stroke hungry herself, takes the Con out of her need for sex. After getting what he asks for at the social level—sex—he pulls the Switch and makes a hasty retreat. His leaving signals, "You're just an easy lay like all the rest." The woman's Payoff is to feel confused, inadequate and NOT OK. Jerry's letdown is his Payoff, which reflects his Adapted Child and the unconscious childhood decision not to be close and that women are NOT OK. To validate this decision, he chooses women with whom he can never be close. So long as the Adapted Child in Jerry remains fearful of intimacy, he will continue this self-defeating, go-nowhere, depressive behavior.

Have Orgasm Will Travel can be a continuing game, as played by Jerry, or a reactive stage as one comes reeling out of a divorce. The latter circumstance most readily fits the situation of the traditionally-married-recently-divorced person, as Guy, who is determined to earn his calling card.

Like most people, Guy lived by a schedule. He arrived at the office at eight every morning, his wife had dinner ready promptly at six, and it was lights out after the 10:00 p.m. news. On Mondays she laundered his shirts and rolled his socks into pairs, and on Saturdays he mowed the lawn while she planned their evening. During the last years of his marriage he occasionally purchased a *Playboy* but never told his wife, much less shared his sexual fantasies. Guy's personality was gray pinstripe.

After his divorce everything familiar collapsed, as did the yardstick he used to measure his personal worth. Aloneness, a strange apartment, shopping, cooking, dirty laundry, socks that didn't match, and unplanned Saturday nights were his legacy.

He spent sleepless nights trying to convince himself that it had happened — he was divorced! At 2:00 a.m. the how's and why's were unimportant as he existed in that unbelievable void created by the absence of that one special person. Nothingness was what he felt as he stared at bare apartment walls and lay in an empty bed. The silence was engulfing. He felt as if his life history had been written on a blackboard *and erased.* Over and over he questioned who he was and who cared. Out of sheer desperation he knew he had to change.

The giant step came one day after work when he stopped by the local "in" place rather than go home to a ghastly T.V. dinner. Feeling scared and awkward, he gulped one drink and left. Once back at the apartment, he surveyed himself in the mirror and decided that he looked pretty trim. The ten pounds he had lost during the past few months hadn't done any harm, and he thought about buying some new clothes to fit his new body.

The next time Guy stopped by the "in" place, he wore tight, faded jeans and a Quiana nylon shirt, unbottoned half-way down just as the clerk had shown him. Less terrified than before, but still feeling uncomfortable, he was surprised when a girl sat down beside him. Bolstered by her interest, he again held counsel with his mirror. He did look good — someone thought so. As he mused over his new image, he wondered if his ex-wife had squelched the real him.

A closet full of tight, faded jeans, Playboy openly dis-played on the coffee table, and tiger print sheets on his king-size playpen announced his entry into singledom. His many months of training paid off as he boasted to his office buddies about the great piece of tail he had last night. Guy had turned hip!

He couldn't bear coming home to an empty apartment. His health suffered and his work suffered. Little sleep, poor eating habits and the energy to live up to page 33 of his sex manual took its toll.

Guy's entry into this game was based on the traditional

Parent tape, "Success as a man is judged on how well you take care of your family." When the yardstick he used (his marriage) to measure his worth was gone, he impulsively grasped another — women and sex. Guy quit traveling when he decided that he didn't have to validate his worth and OKness through women and sexual performance.

He told us, "At that time it was important for me to prove I was a man desired by women. Maybe I was taking one last fling at sowing my wild oats. I don't know for sure, but I do know it was a lot of work!"

SEX WITH YOUR EX

The number of people who have sex with their ex during and after their divorce is astounding. We estimate that 90% have thought about it, 75% have discussed it, and 30% have experienced it.

Many of our workshop participants have commented on the paradox of feeling negative and angry at their ex, while at the same time wanting sex with them. They are afraid to try someone new, and besides, the familiar is easier. Some divorcing couples have had little or no sexual experience with anyone else, and as a result their biology overrides rationality. These motivating forces usually result in short term sexual liaisons. Continued sexual relations between ex-spouses are carried on in the interest of reinforcing some early decisions about oneself and/or the opposite sex. The final product is usually a bad feeling payoff, the purpose of which is to reinforce that decision.

Jill's father was a heavy drinker who, when drunk, became physically abusive toward her mother. Even though her mother had a career and was considered worldly, Jill saw her as weak when it came to dealing with men.

To protect her mother she often manipulated her drunken father into reading her bedtime stories until he passed out on her bed. She feared and hated him, yet held onto the wish that he be loving and kind. When she was six he deserted the family. The altered standard of living, her mother's work which necessitated prolonged absences from the home, and the ruptured fantasy that her father would change intensified her anger and need to construct a defense against a world of harsh, non-caring men.

When she was seven she made three important, yet conflicting, decisions. The first was that *men are unreliable bastards who take advantage of women.* The second was *to grow up and marry a man who would take care of her.* The third was *to have her way with men.*

Jill's conflicting decisions left her yearning for a close protective relationship with a man. However, she was so filled with anger and resentment that genuine intimacy was impossible. She married her Prince Charming who turned out to be much like her father. He was financially unreliable, drank heavily, made promises to change, and in the end deserted her and the children. Jill had unconsciously recreated her original family!

After her divorce she entered the world of work and, like her mother, was successful. However, her personal life was filled with turmoil. Her conflicting decisions about men left her a bitter and sometimes castrating bitch. While the Child in her desired closeness, if a man ventured too close, she would mount an attack and run him off. Then she would ask, "Why do they always leave me?" Her beliefs about men kept her distant, uncommitted and relegated to one night stands and affairs with married men.

Eight months after her divorce, Ted, her ex-husband, made the first of a succession of sporadic appearances which were as consistent as his child support payments. He came expecting and receiving bed, board and an instant family.

For the "sake of the children" and for five years, Jill permitted these visits. Notwithstanding her complaints about his unexpected and often untimely visits, the shirking of his financial responsibilities to the children, and her anger, she slept with him. She justified her behavior by telling herself that she was horny, Ted was available and she might as well use him for something. Because her true, though unconscious, motivation reinforced the belief that men were unreliable and NOT OK, each of these interludes was short-lived and ended with both feeling bad and behaving miserably toward the other.

In their game transaction, Ted's Con was "I'll change and take care of you." Jill bought into the Con out of her wish to be nurtured. When Ted threw the Switch by leaving, Jill felt entitled to her usual bad feeling Payoff which proved her NOT OK beliefs about men.

Jill exited from the game only after getting in touch with her conflicting childhood decisions, which permitted her to see how and why real intimacy with a man was possible. This insight gained through therapy enabled her to make some new decisions about herself and update her perceptions of men. She learned that they weren't all S.O.B.'s and that she had behaved as though they were.

STEPPING STONE

Despite the fear and uncertainty of separation and divorce, if a potential new love is waiting in the wings, the weight of the decision may be lessened. Unfortunately, many new relationships are based on fantasy and poor judgment. The decision to leave your spouse should be based on the quality of that relationship, rather than on the presence of a Mr. or Mrs. Future.

Alice is a beautiful woman in her mid 40's whose two children are grown. Although the last 10 years of her 20-year marriage had been a sham, she remained in an emotionally cool, non-loving marriage "for the children's sake" and because she feared not being able to support herself. Alice blamed her sterile, lifeless marriage on her husband's inability or refusal to be loving and tender. She was partially accurate, but it wasn't the whole story. A look at her childhood will help in understanding her choice of a spouse, why she remained in her marriage, and her entry into a game of "Stepping Stone."

When she was six, her parents divorced after a stormy nine-year marriage. Although she idolized her father, the judge placed Alice and her sister in her mother's custody. Upon leaving the courtroom she spotted her father and excitedly ran to him expecting to be scooped up in his arms, hugged and kissed. Instead, he told her he never wanted to see her again because she had chosen her mother over him.

Alice reacted with chagrin, feelings of abandonment and

guilt. What had she done wrong? She had no voice in the custody decision. Why had she been rejected by the most important person in her life? Her father's distorted black and white view — "You're either with me or against me" — made no sense.

As she grew up she adopted her father's aberrant black and white way of looking at the world. She mistrusted people, particularly men. She questioned her ability to love and be loved. Her distrust grew out of her father's rejection and some early memories about his "odd" behavior. Although she knew little about sex, she had overheard her mother and others make comments about her father's "abnormality" and sensed that he was in some way different. She never saw him again, but in adolescence concluded he was gay.

In her early 20's she married an autocratic man who was emotionally distant and rejecting. Her choice of a husband was consistent with her beliefs about men. Her internal push to be wanted and loved resulted in her first affair. Overwhelmed by guilt, she confessed all to her husband. Another set-up! Her confusion resulted in his distancing even more. Alice interpreted his behavior as one more indication that men, like her father, were harsh, unforgiving, and saw no shades of gray.

Her marriage continued in the same lifeless vein until she met Rick. It was not surprising that she chose a married man who had scores of previous affairs, for a lover. Believing Rick was waiting in the wings, she finally left her husband.

Again, another set-up. Rick was not going to leave his wife and children for her anymore than he did for all his other lovers. Because of her urgent need to be touched, held and desired, which was more intense than her need for actual sex, Rick had another pigeon. Unable to read her own script signals, she used Rick as a "Stepping Stone" out of her marriage into what she naively believed was true romance. The sad and ironic part of Alice's story is that a man capable of an intimate relationship would never choose an emotionally hungry women who needed a man to feel safe, secure and OK with herself.

When his time came for another conquest, and as Rick distanced, she clung ever more tenaciously. Realizing the futility of her situation, she still held on and hurt. It was as if she were proving what she always knew — "men were not to be trusted."

Alice is still clinging to Rick while searching for another to take his place. She is on a merry-go-round, unable to break off one relationship until she finds another. Until she makes contact with and changes her script decisions about men and her feelings of NOT OKness, she will continue to act out her script through her game of "Stepping Stone."

IT REALLY DIDN'T COUNT

Of the myriads of reasons for divorce, affairs are probably the most painful. It is not the sexual encounter itself that is the most crushing; rather, it is the shock and rage over the deceit. Rejection, jealousy, embarrassment, confusion, depression, anger and blame follow in rapid succession. As awareness and feelings merge, perspective is temporarily lost. You question your entire marriage and value system, and frantically search for your inadequacies. You ask yourself, "Where did I fail?"

Enmeshed in this morass of confusion and self-doubt, your thinking becomes muddled. You begin to believe and may act on unreal assumptions — "I am unloved, I am unlovable. Something must be wrong with me." As the anger peaks, you swing from self-pity to murderous thoughts and impulses.

One of the paradoxes of this most painful of events is that the definition of an affair is so illusive. In many ways the ambiguity of meaning is itself one of the culprits. For some, an affair is any kind of clandestine relationship, whether or not physical contact is involved. Others acknowledge an affair only if sexual intercourse has occurred. Kissing, petting, and even oral sex are not included in their definition. Some consider a casual sexual encounter with a prostitute or stranger as simply an event. For them fidelity is retained because of the lack of emotional involvement. Others define an affair as a relationship which involves both the physical and emotional content.

We define an affair as any type of sexual, meaning physical, activity between two consenting adults at least one of whom is married to someone else. Of the many reasons for affairs, these are the most common:

1. AN ESCAPE HATCH . . . Some use alcohol or drugs as a diversion. Others are workaholics and some use sporting sex.

2. A BREAK IN THE DULL ROUTINE . . . If a couple permits the excitement in their relationship to erode, everything, including sex, becomes commonplace and boring. Sex by the clock, Saturday night at 11:00 P.M. when the kids are in bed, is a drag. The familiarity and security that develops in a marriage need not be a romance killer. Instead, it can be the foundation for more imaginative and ardent lovemaking, since each knows what turns the other on. Don't assume that the secrecy and sneakiness of an affair is what makes it exciting. Romance is a quality and creation of the mind, not a set of motel keys.

3. THE PURELY PHYSICAL . . . Some seek sexual relationships devoid of any element of emotional involvement. An emotional problem exists if sexual gratification is enhanced or can only occur under these circumstances. Psychologists have discovered that as a group these people often remark, "The more sex I have with the one I love — the less I love her . . . The more I love her — the less I want sex with her." These feelings reflect an unconscious Parental message about how one should sexually relate to a loved one. It also mirrors the Puritan ethic of the chaste wife whose sole sexual purpose was to bear children to carry on the family name.

4. A SET-UP FOR DIVORCE . . . A husband or wife can set a spouse up to have an affair by being distant and cold. The purpose of the set-up is to get out of the marriage without having to accept responsibility for the divorce. What better or more self-righteous excuse for divorce is there than adultery? Another kind of set-up occurs when the errant spouse "accidentally on purpose" arranges to be found out so that the other will institute the divorce. Again, the errant

spouse is refusing to accept responsibility for initiating the divorce. In many of these cases, neither party is consciously aware of the set-up and underlying motivation.

5. DIFFERENCES IN MORALS AND VALUES ... With the advent of the "Do your own thing" morality, this reason has gained prominence. This can become a significant factor when one of the parties alters his values but neglects to openly inform his spouse of the changed attitudes and beliefs.

6. WRONG PERSON ... You discover that you married the wrong person. Rather than upsetting the apple-cart, you remain in the marriage for the goodies it provides and play around.

7. PARENT AND CULTURAL TAPES ... "The more women you have the better man you are" is a tape common to nearly all of Western Civilization. Little boys are brought up to revere certain women and screw others. This attitude and behavior is so ingrained it almost appears instinctual. Young men know who to "bring home to mother" and who to tell dad about. Many adolescents feel unmanly because of their inability to "score" like the other guys. This attitude can carry over into adulthood and marriage.

8. DEPENDENCY NEEDS ... The need to be needed can exert a tremendous pull as well as being a back-breaking burden. To want to lean on, be cared for and nurtured is a universal and healthy human characteristic. To have internal permission to be dependent allows one to lie back, put his guard down and be close to another human being. The giver and receiver share a sense of mutual closeness and trust which fosters feelings of safety and intimacy.

This delicate balance between giving and receiving is a necessary ingredient for an intimate relationship. If a person has been programmed only to give or only to receive, the scale becomes tipped and the joys of giving and receiving are diminished, if not lost.

Compulsive givers attempt to maintain themselves in a one-up position in order to control, demonstrate their power, and compensate for feelings of NOT OKness. As a result, they seek out partners who are constantly in difficulty and in need of their help. Such people often search out and live with a loser in order to feel like a winner.

This situation is illustrative of the equation ½ + ½ = 1 or, I need you, a ½ in trouble, to make me, a ½ inadequate, feel whole. Marriages based on this equation frequently fail if the dependent one alters his psychological position from NOT OKness to OKness and no longer requires constant care. Should this occur, the giving spouse may re-experience buried feelings of NOT OKness. To avoid these feelings he looks about for another victim to rescue. On the other hand, if the authoritative spouse gives up his rescuer role, the dependent one may experience a rush of fear and seek out another to care for him. In either case the result can be an affair.

In our work with couples teetering on the brink of divorce, we found a wide array of factors which were the real reasons for an affair. These causes, most often unspoken and unconscious, were related to each partner's needs, wants and expectations regarding the other. Ask yourself:

"Do you know when, where, at what time and how I want to lean and be nurtured?" "Do I know myself?"

"Do you know when, where, at what time and how I want you to lean on me?" "Do I know myself?"

"Did I choose an independent, self-reliant spouse only to become resentful when, in the secret way I want, you didn't ask for my help, advice or consent?"

"Did I choose a dependent spouse only to become resentful when you leaned on me?"

Knowing the fine print of the marital contract, particularly in these silent areas, is vital.

For the greater part of their 21-year marriage, Grace and Jim had more than their share of conflicts. However, they loved each other and considered their marriage to be on solid footing. Early in their marriage Jim had an occasional nooner with a secretary, receptionist or cocktail waitress. At first he felt a little guilty and feared that he would be discovered. Since success breeds success, he gained confidence and the frequency of his sexcapades increased. He savored the physical, while telling himself how much more Grace meant to him.

When a friend put Grace onto the truth, she experienced the usual sequence of bad feelings and questioned her personal and sexual worth. She confronted him. Jim replied, "They didn't really count . . . I never cared for them." They counted for Grace — she filed for divorce.

Jim's affairs were based on the belief, "The more you get, the better man you are." Because he never became emotionally involved with these women, he refused to accept responsibility for the divorce.

Irv and Anita's version was somewhat different. For the last 10 of their 15 years of marriage, Irv chased everything in skirts. Despite his ineptness, until the end Anita remained blind to a host of clues even Inspector Clouseau could have detected.

When she could no longer deny the obvious, Anita resorted to resentful silence, fearing the personal, social and financial repercussions of divorce. Eventually she got up the courage to confront Irv, but did so from her Adapted Child ego state. Her child-like manner resulted in Irv's admission, a disclaimer that the others *never really counted,* and a promise to be forever faithful. She crawled back into her world of illusion and believed him.

After several more admissions, pledges to be faithful and, "You're the only one I really love," Anita filed for divorce. Irv became enraged that she would leave a man who truly loved her. After all, his affairs were only matters of the flesh. For two years after their divorce, Anita remained in her Adapted Child available for Irv's Critical Parent putdowns. The ritual they went through during and after after their divorce was a replay of their marital transactions.

A closer look at their personalities revealed that each chose the other as a marriage partner out of weakness. Both dealt with their feelings of inadequacy by finding someone willing and able to fill their voids — Irv to show strength and masculinity and Anita to be taken care of. Even though Anita finally left him, she continued to wonder whether he would have changed if she had remained in the marriage. Her uncertainty about divorcing him was a reflection of her Gimmick, "Am I strong enough to be on my own?" Each time Anita took him back, Irv pulled the Switch by having another affair. Residing beneath his Con, "The others never really counted," lay the ulterior motivation, "I need other women to prove my masculinity."

Another outcome of this kind of sex game occurs when the hurt or victimized party holds onto anger and resentments so tightly that they grow, fester and spill over onto other aspects of his life. Dottie, a 46-year-old divorcee, permitted her anger over her ex-husband's affairs to erode her trust in all men. In nearly every interaction with a man she came across as bitchy and hard. She expected the worst, behaved that way, and her prophecy never went unfulfilled. Dottie's anger toward the world eventually reached such proportion that not infrequently she became the third party in a marital triangle. Upon entering an affair she told herself, "People can't be trusted and feelings don't count."

99 WAYS TO LEAVE YOUR LOVER

The Toxic Toms and Poisonous Pattys of this world con the shirt off your back while telling you how much better off you are without one. They have the uncanny ability to enlist your aid in the pursuit of their own pleasures, even at your expense. Their seeming concern for your welfare, and their skill in handing out phony strokes like they were gum drops give them temporary credibility. The marital and after divorce games played by these people are at the second and third degree level and are emotionally and/or physically dangerous.

Tom and Pam had four years of fun, travel, financial success and three children. They had nine more years of sheer hell along with two more children. During the last years of their marriage, Tom was a bastard. Physical abuse was only part of the picture as he embarrassed and verbally abused Pam in the presence of others, particularly women.

Tom was a good-looking man who dressed and carried himself with an air of self-confidence and sophistication. In most situations he was the center of attention, yet he didn't actively call attention to himself. He was adept at reading people — if there was a woman who was feeling down and in need of stroking he could pick her out of a crowd. He knew how to make others feel good in his presence.

This combination of quiet strength, assuredness, ability to listen, stroke and read people invited others to want to know him better. Women saw these qualities as sensuous and sexy. The aura which emanated from him was, "You're fortunate to know me." When his facade wore thin, he was able to sustain relationships with women by falling back on a little boy quality which hooked into their Nurturing Parent.

In the first years of his marriage, Tom performed his husbandly duties admirably, with but a dash of extracurricular activity. By the sixth year he was constantly into drugs, debt and other women's pants. Despite his late night escapades, DWI (driving while intoxicated) convictions and abudant evidence of unfaithfulness, Pam kept herself blind to what was happening.

On the many occasions she saw him making open advances to other women, he would reassure her with, "Believe me baby, you're the only one I want. You're the greatest in bed." So flagrant was her self-deception, that when she contracted gonorrhea she convinced herself that she had picked it up in a public restroom. This was the 94th way, yet she stayed.

When 99 rolled around even Pam couldn't hide from reality. Tiring of their quarrels, Tom moved in with Jane, who was, in many ways, the mirror image of Pam. She pulled him out of scrapes, bailed him out of jail, paid his debts and accepted his abuse. Like Pam she believed that she was the one who could help him reach his true potential. Unfortunately, the only thing Jane learned was her limits for frustration and abuse.

Tiring of the hassles with Jane and with a bucket of Pam's tears to grease the way, he returned home. It didn't take a Jimmy the Greek to predict that the dètènte would be short-lived. Within six months Tom left with a sweet young thing 15 years his junior. Living a hand to mouth existence, with no financial help for her or the kids, Pam finally divorced Tom.

Now it was sweet young thing's turn. Like any good mother she cared for her *man-child* even to the point of posting his bail for non-support. Last we heard, sweet young thing was sour, aging and angry as hell! Not only was she helping support his kids, she also had to care for Tom's latest gift, their infant son. Tom had little time or interest in grumbling housewives and mothers and was soon out searching for a woman who could really love and appreciate him.

That women were attracted to Tom was quite understandable. They wished to be desired by an intelligent, good-looking, sexy man whose potential they saw as enormous. Tom's Con was, "With a good looking woman like you I can make it big." All believed they held that special bit of magic which would enable him to rise to the top. This was their Gimmick. Tom pulled the Switch by leaving when they had served their purpose and he found another who could offer him more. Notice, he always had a woman around. Tom can't make it alone — in truth he is dependent on women.

The best way to deal with a Toxic Tom or Poisonous Patty is to heed Mother's warning, "Don't talk to strangers who *promise* you candy."

DRY GAMES

The relative subtlety of dry sex games, those in which intercourse does not occur, helps account for the fact that the sexual aspect often eludes our awareness. These games can be as emotionally and physically dangerous as wet games if they are allowed to escalate to the third degree.

STITCHES

The main thrust of Stitches is to get your ex temporarily back under your roof to taunt and get back at him through sex . . . "Look, but don't touch!" There are many variations of

Stitches, such as Migraine, Root Canal, Surgery, Boob Lift, etc. In each instance the disabled ex, typically the ex-wife because she has custody, manages to get Mr. Ex back into the house for a night or two to help care for the children.

On the surface her reasons seem legitimate. But are they? Granted Mrs. Ex may be temporarily out of commission, but could she have arranged for some other source of aid? Could the children have stayed with Mr. Ex while she recuperates? The presence of a game transaction rests on the answers to these questions. In other words, is she using her incapacitation and the children to draw him back, even if only briefly? The degree to which the game becomes sexualized depends on the motives and moves.

During their marriage Sam admired and frequently commented to Dora on the size and shape of other women's breasts. Although he never directly put Dora down for her small breasts, his message was loud and clear. After their divorce Dora decided to have a breast implant to enlarge and reshape her breasts. Several days before the surgery she called a much surprised Sam to tell him of her decision and made "noises" about needing transportation to and from the hospital. Taken aback and feeling somewhat stunned, he volunteered.

As they were weaving their way through traffic enroute to the hospital, she told how him difficult it would be, at least for the first few days, to care for herself and the children. Sam offered to help. The next shocker was Dora's suggestion that he stay over for a couple of nights since it would be more convenient. Feeling uneasy with the idea, though unable to deny her logic, he agreed.

With the kids in bed and Dora propped up against several pillows, she asked if he wouldn't be more comfortable sharing her king size bed rather then sleeping on a lumpy couch. She reassured him that her concern was for his well-being and that it was quite all right. As with her first suggestion he felt awkward, but since part of him still wanted her he agreed.

For the next several days Sam took care of the kids and doctored Dora. He attended to her needs, even helping cleanse an infection which developed in her stitches. Like a couple of five-year olds, they played doctor and patient touching and looking.

Although overt sex never entered the picture, Dora got her point across, "Look, touch, but you can't have; Ha Ha." Sam left feeling confused, angry and put upon. He wasn't exactly sure what had happened. From that point on their relationship deteriorated. Sam never caught on that the entire transaction was calculated for Dora to get in the last word. The game permitted her to end their relationship in a top dog position.

Another variant of Stitches is, "I'm Gonna Get My Tubes Tied." Frequently this is Mrs. Ex's way of letting Mr. Ex know that she has become more available for sex and that her previous atitudes, feelings, and behaviors in the sexual realm have changed. This can be a super-charged game transaction if, when they were married, their behavior and attitudes about sex were dominated by traditional Parent tapes.

Stitches can escalate to the third degree level if Mr. Ex temporarily moves in to care for Mrs. Ex and acts on his sexual fantasies stimulated by Mrs. Ex's behavior. If he makes a sexual advance and she backs off protesting her innocence, the transaction can end in an attempted or actual rape or murder.

This kind of game can be avoided if, in the beginning, Mr. Ex shifts into his Adult and ask himself, "Why is she telling me this?" The Adult answer has to be "It's no longer my business if she has her tubes tied."

FRIGID MAN

You're single and can come and go as you please. You are free to see and be with several women without fear of hassle. In your married days you may have envied that guy who was forever on the make and "scoring" with every available woman. You probably thought, "Boy, what a life!" Now that you are divorced, you become acutely aware of the myths surrounding bachelorhood. You wince when your married buddies pump you for information with that sly, you lucky dog expression on their faces.

Parts of your new lifestyle are fun and rewarding. You like the freedom to make and alter your schedule without being forever accountable, and you especially savor the female smorgasbord. You also encounter another aspect of singleness you hadn't considered, *diminished structure and predictability.* Knowing when, how and with whom saves energy and provides you with a sense of security.

In the sexual realm one of the most difficult decisions a recently separated or divorced person must make is the with whoms, hows, whens, and whats of sex. When you were married you knew what each liked, wanted and was willing to do. The approach, technique and timing were relatively predictable. If you married young, your sex tapes may never have been examined as you followed along under the protective umbrella of tradition.

Remove this structure, this scaffolding of experience, and you are left with a measure of newness which, more often than not, is experienced as fear and uncertainty. Not only are you unsure of society's expectations, you're even more baffled by those of your new partner and your ability to satisfy them. The older you are, the greater your confusion and unassuredness. You have been out of circulation longer and your ideas about sex are less in tune with present day standards and modes of conduct.

During his 25 years of marriage, Barry worked hard and became a charter member of the establishment, owned a successful business and reared three kids. From the outside his marriage to Rhonda seemed solid as a rock. From the inside it felt as hard and unyielding.

Sex for Barry and Rhonda was good, but infrequent. For years he lived with that familiar aching sensation in his loins, though he remained a faithful husband. Following his divorce Barry learned some astonishing things about himself, women, and sex, which confused and startled him. He was amazed that women considered him attractive and very much the catch. Another surprise was the open and direct manner in which some women approached and pursued him. While on one hand he was put off by their assertiveness, on the other he thoroughly enjoyed the attention which fed his ego.

The Critical Parent part of his personality considered these women crude and beneath him, while the Child in him enjoyed the forbidden fruit.

These conflicting and diverse desires resulted in an intense internal clash. Should he or shouldn't he? Barry's outdated sex tapes, his inexperience in relating to a new breed of sexually assertive women, his yearning for the forbidden and questioning whether or not he'd be able to match up, more often than not left him sexually impotent. While he enjoyed the physical contact and satisfied his partners orally and manually, seldom could he achieve and sustain an erection sufficient for intercourse. In his after divorce sex life, he was living by outdated messages about women and sex. He wanted something different, but never gave himself permission to act according to his present needs, wants and fantasies. With or without Rhonda, he remained sexually frustrated.

His impotence was related to his ideas about sex and how women *should* behave. This was demonstrated by the fact that on the three occasions he had "Sex With Your Ex" he was sexually competent. However, when he slept with sexually assertive women, his Critical Parent sprang to life attacking his Child ego state with statements like, "You're not supposed to act like that," or "You're lying with a whore."

The game escalated when he established a sexual relationship with a younger woman who was free and demonstrative about the pleasures of sex. The more erotically she behaved, the more frigid Barry became. He shared his difficulties with her and she agreed to be understanding and patient. Her patience lasted six months before her frustration spilled over onto other aspects of their relationship and she began withdrawing both personally and sexually. They soon broke up.

In Barry's version of "Frigid Man," his Con was "I'm ready and available for erotic, fun sex." When a woman came on sexy, Barry became frightened, impotent and pulled the Switch with, "You're acting like a whore." His bad feeling Payoff was anger and fear.

Until Barry updates his sex tapes so they fit his present

needs and wants, he will remain conflicted, impotent and frustrated. His second option is to alter his sexual desires and behavior so they more comfortably fit with his Parent tapes.

MEET MARY

Should I see her? Should I talk to him? I'd like to strangle her but I still want to sleep with her. Should I go over and talk about the kids and then maybe, just for tonight, make love? Maybe she's with someone else? During the separation and right after divorce, these confusing and conflicting questions, thoughts and desires ricochet in our heads.

As you emotionally unhook, the amount of contact you want or believe you need changes. For some, the initial feelings of rejection result in rage and withdrawal. For others, the opposite holds true. They yearn, want and cling to each other much like a life support system.

Over time and with reintegration of themselves as separate, independent and fully functioning people, they feel little or no *push* to see, be with or have any unnecessary contact with their ex. Rather than experience a *push* for contact or withdrawal, they can live with prolonged absence or interact without emotional pain.

Jealousy is a strong emotion, and if escalated to the third degree it usually hits the headlines of your newspaper. The following dry sex games (Meet Mary, See How Popular I Am, I Don't Want To Meet John, Paul Revere) are variations of the same theme, each using jealousy to obtain the final Payoff. Meet Mary is a two handed game drawing in a new love interest through story telling. Sex is only a ploy. The real issue is control or "who's in charge of whom?"

In their marriage Merv was considered the strong one. He was direct, assertive and on the boisterous side. However, he relied heavily on Carol's opinion and seldom acted without checking with her first. Carol was very much the woman behind the man. She enjoyed being needed and readily accepted her behind-the-scene role.

During their separation Merv began calling, filling Carol in on his new life. Carol was a willing listener and responded with encouragement and support. Their conversations proceeded from the social to the sexual as he shared his problems, exploits and new sexual techniques. On occasion he subtly offered to show her what he had learned. Carol passed over these remarks, since she maintained her one-up position by remaining just out of arms reach. If they had sex she would jeopardize her upper hand.

After passing through the Patty Cake phase, Merv settled into a relationship with Mary. Nevertheless, he continued calling Carol, telling her how his thoughts about her interfered with his sexual potency with Mary. Merv placed Carol in the top dog position and she willingly accepted.

As he settled into a dependent Child-Parent relationship with Mary and broke his symbiotic ties to Carol, the tone of their conversations changed. He related his new found self-confidence, the "joys of sex" with Mary and occasionally asked how she was getting along. As Merv transferred his dependency to Mary, Carol began feeling left out, resentful and jealous.

One evening he suggested she meet him and Mary for a drink. Carol exploded, "I don't care about her! Why in the hell would I want to meet HER?" Merv flipped into his Critical Parent, coming back with, "I always knew you were petty and jealous!"

Merv's Con was, "I'll share my new life with you." His secret message was, "I'll make you jealous by telling you about my sex life." Carol's Gimmick was listening in order to be in the top dog controlling position. When Carol refused to meet Mary, Merv threw the Switch with accusations, which was his way of saying, "I got you, ha ha . . . I'm more powerful than you!" His Payoff was indignation and righteous anger, which put him in control and permitted *him* to make the final break. Her Payoff was resentment, jealousy and confusion. Had they emotionally unhooked and given up the symbiotic Child-Parent relationship that existed in their marriage, the game could have been avoided.

This letter from a reader of "After Divorce" illustrates the various forms "Meet Mary" takes. What does this letter tell you about the couple and the nature of their after divorce relationship?

"I couldn't believe it, but my ex-husband called and asked to borrow an evening wrap for his date. When I said, "No," he got very hateful and called me a jealous bitch.

I know he's not dumb so he must be crazy. What do I do?"

SEE HOW POPULAR I AM

Greg's parents were totally immersed in their careers. Their idea of fun was a quiet evening at home reading the latest professional journals. Greg, an only child, felt like a satellite in orbit rather than a part of a family. His wish that his parents would get involved in Little League or Boy Scouts remained unfulfilled.

His parents' lack of involvement led to feelings of rejection, a questioning of his personal worth, and a decision to prove to himself and others that he was worthy of attention and recognition. Greg operated out of a NOT OK life position, and as an adult compensated for these feelings by working extremely hard at everything he did. His life equation was *Firstness = OKness.* It was impossible always to be first, so each second or third was taken as a failure. While to the casual onlooker he appeared self-assured and confident, his perceptions and feelings about himself were just the opposite. The slightest rejection could throw him into a depression or rage.

Somehow Greg and Peggy endured a 10-year marriage and had two kids before Peggy called it quits. Greg used normal feelings of grief and sadness to reinforce his NOT OKness. Out of his lowly concept of self and inability to tolerate rejection, he set up a *get back at* game. He used sex, "See How Popular I Am With Other Women," to make Peggy jealous.

Greg became the swingingest, best-dressed bachelor in town. He bought a posh townhouse, gave some extravagant parties, and frequented the finest restaurants and clubs. However, there were a couple of flies in the ointment! His new friends put the almighty dollar ahead of him, and Peggy wasn't aware of his new life style.

Poor Greg! He found it necessary to play two-handed and invited Peggy to play along. He began calling and inquiring how she was doing. He managed to fit into the conversations, "The damn maid still hasn't cleaned up the mess from the party Janet and I threw the other night," or, "We had a blast at the disco last night . . . met some sharp dancers." His ploys became more overt with statements like, "I won't be able to have the kids this weekend because a woman will be here . . . don't you agree that the kids shouldn't be around when someone is staying over?" Occasionally he even had a girlfriend pick up the children. As calculating as this appears, most of the Gregs of this world are unaware of their motivation and would wax with indignation if accused of attempting to *get her* on purpose.

Greg's Con was, "How Are You Doing?" The ulterior motivation was, "I'll Tell You About Me and Make You Jealous." Peggy hooked into the game out of her Gimmick, "I'm Still Interested." After a number of such conversations, Peggy blew up and told Greg to shove it. Greg's Switch was to reply innocently, "I'm not going to talk to you if you're going to act like that." Greg exited feeling put upon and righteously indignant. Peggy's Payoff was confusion, anger and jealousy.

Peggy could have cut the game off at its inception by assertively stating that she wasn't going to listen to any of his stories or questions. Greg could have done likewise had he been aware of his NOT OK life position, which led to attempts to prove that he was number one — more desired by the opposite sex.

The following letter is an example of a second degree "See How Popular I Am" game escalating to the third degree:

> "My ex-husband has visitation with my children every other Sunday. Since our divorce he has made a practice of openly talking to our young children about his love affairs and goes to the extreme of showing the kids pictures of these women taken on his bed.
>
> I have confronted him, and he calls his own kids liars. I don't think he should be allowed visitation until he gets his life straightened out. Don't you agree that I should take him to court?"

I DON'T WANT TO MEET JOHN

When Beth and Alex divorced, Beth's main complaint was that Alex controlled her. When they first married, Beth was very much the homemaker. She delighted in *taking care of* Alex and their two sons, and was devoted to her home. As Beth involved herself in the personal growth and feminist movements, her attitudes and behavior began to change. While she still cared for her family, she wanted more for herself.

Alex was an easygoing guy whose main extracurricular activity was watching Monday Night Football. During the three years in which Beth underwent her metamorphosis, Alex felt confused, neglected and rejected. Their arguments were few, but the tension and silent anger created a steel curtain between them. While he wanted Beth to be happy and involved, he felt that there were limits as to what she should and should not do. At the time of their separation, each felt manipulated and controlled by the other. She called him a "male chauvinist pig," and he retorted with "libber."

Name calling accomplished little and explained nothing. What happened was that the implied and unspoken rules governing their marriage had changed. They married under one set of roles and expectations and divorced under another.

A couple of years after their divorce, Alex came to one of our workshops and reported that Beth still complained about his control over her, and he still felt manipulated by her. Since the issue of control was a long standing thorn in the marriage, Beth's involvement in social causes and her changed role expectations were not the primary causes of the divorce. At most they had a facilitative effect.

We asked Alex to relate the last time Beth accused him of controlling her. He reported, "As usual, if I was going to pick the kids up later or earlier than expected, I'd call ahead. Because of a late appointment, I left word with my oldest son that I'd be about thirty minutes late. Just as I was leaving the office, Beth called angrier than hell! She told me she was sick and tired of me controlling her life and she would no longer protect me from meeting her dates. I was dumbfounded! How was I to know she was arranging her schedule around me?"

This incident was but a replay of one of their marital conflicts. Alex would state a position (which Beth accepted), only to change the position somewhere down the line. The changed attitude or belief was seldom communicated in words, but rather by his behavior.

Early in the separation Alex was in intense emotional pain and angrily exclaimed, "I never want to see you with another man." Despite the inappropriateness, if not impossibility, of this request Beth agreed. She began by arranging her social and dating schedule so that Alex never bumped into any of her male friends. This included those times Alex came to pick up the children. As her circle of friends and social activities widened, she found it increasingly difficult to juggle her schedule around Alex's.

Over the next two years, and as Alex emotionally detached, he no longer needed this kind of protection. Although he never retracted his request, his behavior and what she had learned from mutual friends communicated his new decision. Being the nurturer she was and still feeling guilty over divorcing him, she ignored the new information and continued to act upon his early request.

Neither looked at present realities. Alex failed to see Beth's social contortions, which were readily visible, and she paid little attention to his change in behavior and attitude. Instead, the harder she worked to comply, the angrier and more controlled she felt.

Had either read the other's behavior, asked a question, or verbalized a new decision, two years of anger and frustration could have been avoided. Beneath Alex's Con, "I don't want to meet John," lay the secret message, "Let's pretend you're not sleeping with anyone else." Beth's Gimmick was, "I feel guilty ... he's so hurt and he needs my protection." Two years later Alex pulled the Switch with "You dummy, what are you pretending for?" The game ended with both collecting identical bad feelings — righteous indignation, anger and feelings of being controlled.

PAUL REVERE

How many of you have simmered to the boiling point as you thought of him or her out with someone else? How often have you feigned concern over the children as an excuse to berate her for going out *too* much? How often have you popped by unexpectedly to see the kids when your real reason was to *check up* on her? How many of you don't really give a damn what she's doing so long as she's home, alone and miserable? Paul Revere players act out their jealous anger by checking up on their ex or ex-to-be. They may do this even if they are *in* love, *in* hate, or *in* anger. Their refusal or inability to emotionally detach increases their separation distress and consequent feelings of aloneness and emptiness. These are the building blocks for a game of Paul Revere.

Charlie is a single-handed, first degree Paul Revere player who had worn blinders to the deteriorating state of his marriage. When Barbara filed for divorce Charlie became remorseful, angry and loving all in the same breath. For the first few months after separating, he remained intensely attached to her. Whenever he was in, about, or around the neighborhood he drove by to have a "look-see." As he cruised up the street toward the house, he could feel his heart pound and his palms begin to sweat.

He didn't know exactly what to look for, and even if he did he wouldn't know what to do. After several passes he devised a plan. He'd check to see whether or not the lights were on, her car was in the driveway and if the newspaper had been picked up. While part of him hoped he'd find a sign that she was home, another part wished she was out so that he could fuel his jealous anger.

As his sleuthing continued he began feeling foolish, futile, and cornered. If her car was in the driveway, he'd imagine that she was shacking up at *his* place. If her car wasn't in the driveway, he'd torment himself with the thought that she had parked it in the garage and *they* were sleeping in *his* bed. Since Barbara had a timer on the house lights, he could only imagine what this clue meant. Backed into a corner, his anger intensified; nonetheless, he continued his futile vigil.

While in his corner, Charlie pulled the Switch on himself. Regardless of what he saw, he came up with another theory about the facts and bathed in his Payoff of jealous anger and rejection. His only way out of the corner he had created was to emotionally unhook and detach himself from Barbara's new life. Thank goodness this game is short-lived. If it wasn't our streets would be littered with exes causing midnight traffic jams.

A harder second degree version of Paul Revere draws in the ex-spouse. Playing at this level, Charlie might confront Barbara with his suspicions and accuse her of sleeping around, leaving the children alone, and being irresponsible.

Playing at the third degree level, Charlie might unexpectedly stop by late one evening and confront Barbara and her date. Such a confrontation could result in a fist fight, calling in the cops, or one of the parties being seriously injured or killed.

———————————————————

After reading these case histories you may be asking yourself, "Because I'm divorced should I be celibate? When, where and with whom can I have game-free sex?"

You can begin answering these questions by making a script checklist. Some key points are:

1. Did your parents openly display affection toward one another?
2. What did they tell you about sex?
3. How did they tell you?
4. How do you imagine each of your parents thought, felt and acted with sex?
5. How did you first learn about sex and what was your initial reaction?
6. What is your sex life position about men — about women — about yourself?
7. Have you used sex to get something else? If so, for what and how often?

Your answers to these questions make up many of your present beliefs and attitudes about sex — in other words, your sexual script.

We offer the following suggestions for those of you re-entering the single world.

1. Meet people first — NOT a man or a woman.
2. When involving yourself in a new dating relationship, make a no-sex contract for a specified period of time.

This will enable you to get to know the person as a human being rather than simply as a sexual object.

3. Don't have sex with your ex.

4. Don't permit yourself to become so stroke deprived that you become a weak battery.

5. If you feel guilty or uncomfortable with your sexual behavior, either change your behavior to fit your values or alter your values to fit your behavior.

5

TEETER-TOTTER

The period of separation is one of fear, illusion, confusion, disillusionment and contradiction. What you do with a feeling is equally as important as, if not more important than, the feeling itself. You can immobilize yourself with fear or be fearful and still move on. You can do more than one thing at a time!

Fear and Illusion

A portion of the fear is very real and based upon a myriad of personal and financial unknowns. The remainder is more a reflection of one's personality and life script than external reality.

Many dreams, hopes and fears about being single again are founded on illusions. Some are positive and hopeful. Others are filled with terror, self-doubt and dread. For some the promise of singledom is rapidly fulfilled. For most the pain and dislocation are far greater than they anticipated. Dealing with children, friends, dating, sex, money and the joys and problems of daily living can take on exciting, yet frightening aspects, as you plunge into these responsibilities 24 hours a day, seven days a week.

Confusion

Confusion is born out of the rapid and often uncontrolled changes taking place within you, your children and your spouse. When you separate you become different! Your personal identity, social status, and ways of perceiving and thinking trigger change, the result of which you can only know with time. Some describe this period as "spinning like a top!"

Disillusionment

Detaching from the *marital system* can be as difficult as detaching from a spouse. The marital system was as much a part of your life as your spouse. A year or two after the divorce you may only faintly miss the person, yet long for the ordered predictability that characterized the marriage.

As you try on new roles and ideas, you find yourself yearning for the old. Those taken-for-granted inconsequentials suddenly loom with monumental importance. One woman told us, "I was shocked when the banker treated me differently as Mrs. Betty Smith than he had when I was Mrs. John Smith. I had lost my status, and yet I was the same me." Another woman reported, "He always brought me my morning coffee in bed. I never thought about it, much less appreciated it. Now I miss it."

One depressed fellow exclaimed, "It was Penny who called the babysitters, planned the parties and made our tennis court reservations. I didn't know she was responsible for taking care of my needs to that extent." A man divorcing after 25 years summarized his separation, "I am a part-timer. I'm the old me part-time and the new me part-time. I cook part-time and eat out part-time. I see my kids part-time and I'm lonely part-time. Now I'm even impotent part-time."

Contradictions

During separation the contradictions in feelings and behavior can be so overwhelming as to set you on an emotional see-saw! You may find yourself saying one thing and doing another only to reverse your position the next hour, day or week. Monday you may never want to see her again, and on Tuesday seeing her is the most important thing in your life. You may desperately want him and at the same time covet angry or even murderous thoughts. On Wednesday you feel up, powerful and self-reliant. On Thursday you feel down, alone and helpless. This love/hate teeter-totter is so confusing and exhausting that many believe they are going crazy.

Most of us who have lived through this look back and say, "Why in the hell did I do that?" You may even laugh at some of the ridiculous things you said, did and thought. One man told us, "People gave me some good advice which I listened to but didn't really hear." Another said, "I was told to protect myself financially, but I never believed it was necessary." One woman divorcing after 19 years stated, "I discounted advice and suggestions thinking he wouldn't do that to me. The S.O.B. did!"

It is understandable why so many couples reconcile during this love/hate phase as they swing from, "I've got to start over at 35 . . . 40 . . . 45" to, "Hell, I can't let it all go down the drain."

The turmoil created by these contradictory thoughts, actions, and feelings leaves you vulnerable and aching for stability and familiarity. As a result, rehooking back into old or creating new games with your ex-to-be is increased. While the content of the new games may be different, they reflect old marital conflicts.

HOUSE KEY

Jenny and Doug have the legal wheels of their divorce in high gear. Jenny helped Doug move into his new apartment and doled out his share of sheets, towels and the leftover Melmac dishes. Theirs was to be a civilized divorce!

It was so civilized that Doug popped by the house at will. He mowed the lawn, recaulked the bathtub and played ball with the boys. Some Saturdays he came by to fix breakfast even before Jenny and the kids were up.

On occasion Jenny had the fleeting thought that Doug would have to stop letting himself in as if he still lived there. Since their Parent tapes about men and women, husbands and wives, and role expectations were similar, she accepted his behavior along with the manly tasks he so willingly performed. In marriage both had accepted the traditional models of the weaker passive female and the stronger protective male. Each defined his own personhood, sexuality, and role in terms of the other. For Jenny womanhood was tied into the roles of wife and mother. For Doug manhood was equated with being a father and provider.

A further reason that both accepted Doug's free access to the home was that it provided some measure of protection from the separation distress they were experiencing. When Doug didn't know where to go or what to do, he could always go over and mow the lawn. Jenny accepted Doug's presence not only for the tasks he performed, but also because his presence was familiar and therefore reassuring.

Nonetheless, Jenny began experiencing Doug's comings and goings as intrusions. Her silent approval changed to silent anger, which escalated with each visit. When she awoke one Saturday morning to find Doug sprawled out on the floor watching T.V. with the kids, she exploded and demanded not only that he leave but also give her the house key. Doug looked at her innocently, shuffled out the door muttering, "What a bitch! After all I've done for her, *she* kicks me out."

Jenny's Con was not asking for the key in the beginning. Her ulterior motive was, "I don't want to give up being taken care of." Doug didn't relinquish the key voluntarily because of his feelings of aloneness and desire to hold onto his role of father and provider. Jenny blamed Doug for her predicament and pulled the Switch by becoming angry and lashing out at him. Her Payoff was justifiable anger and his was surprise, rejection, defeat and anger.

The key, that avenue to the house which gave access to a familiar world of people, transactions and material objects, was also a symbol used to reinforce their Parental tapes as well as to reduce their separation distress. Jenny initiated the game by not asking for the key, thereby permitting Doug free access to the house. Doug willingly played along in order to hold onto the marital system and deny the reality of the separation. Neither understood what had happened as they took the transaction at face value.

Some women consciously withhold asking for the key out of fear. They fear hurting their spouse—after all, it was once his house, too, and they imagine how strange he must feel having to ring the doorbell. Many fear a confrontation, especially if a settlement hasn't been reached. Some fear managing the house and children alone or that he might abandon the children. As long as he has the key, some degree of contact is assured.

These concerns provide the breeding ground for a game of "House Key." As soon after the separation as possible, preferably the same or next day, the issue of the key should be addressed, discussed and resolved. If the one leaving the marital residence refuses to relinquish it, have the locks changed. While the emotional impact and initial response may be harsh, over the long haul the results will be in both parties' best interests.

You can handle the key in one of five ways:

1. Don't ask for it and feel persecuted, angry and resentful.
2. Don't ask now and explode later.
3. Ask from your Adapted Child (passive and weak position) and invite a Critical Parent, "No!"
4. Demand from your Critical Parent and instigate a fight.
5. Ask, at the time of separation, from your Adult. If refused, change the locks.

Giving up the key is a major and threatening step for both parties. It is one of the first steps toward detachment, independence and acceptance of the divorce.

IT'S MINE . . . NO, IT'S MINE

At its simplest, property division is complicated even if you only own *three* books. Difficulties can arise because:

1. Each views the settlement through his own eyes.
2. Symbolic meanings are attached to money and property.
3. Division of property can be used as a weapon to hurt or threaten, or as a way to gain independence.

Differing Points of View

Each of us sees and interprets things and events from our own perspective. Even when a couple attempts to deal with each other honestly, differences of opinion almost always occur. In most divorces at least one claims that he got the short end. Although some people do get the short end, this claim usually reflects disappointment in not getting one's way.

A fifteen-acre parcel of land, if appropriately developed, may have the potential of tripling in value. However, if you have little time, skill or financial resources to develop the property, its value to you may be considerably less than that $15,000 Certificate of Deposit sitting in the safe deposit box. For you, one $15,000 bird-in-the-hand is worth more than three $15,000 birds-in-the-bush.

Symbolic and Sentimental Value

As discussed in Chapter Three, money is more than a medium of exchange for goods and services. Its symbolic meanings are multifold. The same holds true for possessions. Any lawyer will tell you that it is difficult, if not impossible, to place a specific dollar value on many items, due to the personal and sentimental value people attach to them. While a $900 antique clock may have little meaning to Mr. X., he may fight for his well-worn easy chair whose worth, when new, may only have been $350.

Many a person has spent as much, if not more, in time and attorney's fees to retain a possession because of the psychological meaning they attach to it. This is more likely to occur if the person has put a great deal of him- or herself into obtaining or building the object.

Bill, a lover of old cars, spent nearly three years restoring an automobile whose worth in the marketplace was between $3500 and $4000. He considered it only fair that he receive the car in the settlement. Since he lived in a community property state and his ex-to-be viewed the car solely in terms of dollars and cents, she wanted her fair share. Bill perceived the car as an extension of himself and placed a higher and personal value on it. Aware of Bill's emotional investment in the car, she used it as her trump card to effect a trade-off for a far more expensive item.

Weapon

Not infrequently one of the parties in a hotly contested divorce attempts to emotionally and/or financially hurt the other. In these instances it is vital that, at the time of the separation, all possessions be inventoried and a legal instrument effected which prevents the transfer, spending, or hiding of assets.

Although transferring or hiding assets tend to be a man's tactic particularly if he owns his own business, women also have their methods. In the above example Bill's wife used the symbolic significance of the car as a weapon to obtain a more expensive possession.

Independence

While both men and women experience intense stress over the breakup of the marriage, more often than not, it is the woman who is more affected by the financial aspects. The difference stems from the fact that many women have little or no occupational experience to fall back on. While Mr. X may find himself in a tight financial pinch, he is already employed and his occupational experience makes him a more salable employment commodity. What man after 15 or more years of marriage finds it necessary after divorce to start work at the bottom of the ladder? A woman who spent most of her adult life as a mother and housewife will, in all likelihood, feel naked and financially unprepared to care for and meet her future financial needs and wants. A woman in this position will view the settlement as her lifeline to financial security.

At the other extreme some men and women place themselves in the most tenuous of financial situations in order to "get out." Ken, a businessman of moderate means, lived a life of hell as his wife carried on affair after affair. Like the good martyr, he remained in the marriage until his daughters left for college. He claimed that he hated his wife, yet he was willing to give her everything except his pension in order to get out quickly and quietly. Since his children are of age and he lives in a community property non-alimony state, this is blatantly ruinous. If he hates her, one has to wonder why he is so willing to give her everything. Is his freedom under these circumstances in the service of maintaining his martyred victim position?

In Randy's version of "It's Mine . . . No It's Mine" pay attention to how he used a stereo as his vehicle to stay mad, martyred and hurt.

Randy built and loved an intricate, sophisticated sound system which he perceived as an extension of himself. When they separated, Janice demanded that everything in the house be left intact so the children would have an un-disrupted environment. She continually reminded Randy that his earning potential was greater and he would soon be able to recoup his loses. Since he still loved Janice, wanted the best for his children, and wasn't thinking clearly, he passively accepted her demands.

As the divorce entered its final stages, Randy's anger peaked and he demanded possession of the stereo. He spent an additional $500 in attorney's fees attempting to gain custody of the stereo. He lost! Had he negotiated at the onset of the separation he might have been successful and avoided additional attorney's fees. Since his life script was based on self-sacrifice, the fact that he sabotaged himself was not sur-prising.

Three years later Randy still uses this loss to feel bad. Everytime he sees or hears a fine piece of sound equipment, he exclaims with a sad soulful look, "I used to have a better one." It is as if he wants Janice to feel bad whenever she plays the stereo. However, she has thoroughly enjoyed listening to the set and is unaware of the internal single-handed game Randy is playing.

Randy uses a portable radio, though he could afford another stereo. The bottom line is his unwillingness to leave the past behind and an unconscious desire to remain the hopeless, angry victim.

There are so many others besides the principals waiting ready to play "It's Mine . . . No It's Mine," that this game has become institutionalized. Divorce is a multimillion dollar business! Some lawyers, and we emphasize some, enter the game exclaiming, "No, it's mine too," their payoff being a fat fee.

One recent development is the use of arbitrators. While an attorney is needed to handle legal matters, an arbitrator can aid in ironing out personal differences which pertain to property. The advantage of an arbitrator is that his fee is less and he is an objective third party. This objectivity changes the psychological attitude of the proceedings from an adversary, get him/her orientation, to one of mutual satisfaction of dif-ferences.

IN THE NAME OF . . .

During the last two decades the Growth and Human Potential Movements have spread across the country with such vitality that all of us in some way have been touched. It seems that everyone wants to do his own thing, to come out of the closet and to be recognized. With few exceptions, we agree with causes which increase personal and social freedoms. However, as with most innovations, some people misconstrue or misuse their intended meaning.

The Women's Liberation movement is a case in point. It has been made the scapegoat for endless personal and social ills. Many have blamed the phenomenally increasing rate of divorce on Women's Liberation. While we do not see a strict cause and effect relationship between the two, we believe there is a correlation between divorce and changes in role expectations.

Many women want out of the box our culture has created. However, we have seen and worked with women who have thrown the baby out with the bath water! Rather than utilize new skills to help bring about a better marital relationship, which includes personal growth, out of stored up anger and frustration, they opt for divorce, equating it with freedom and liberation.

We challenge the belief that freedom is a necessary consequence of divorce. Independence, freedom, and liberation are as much a function of how you structure and manage your life as your marital status. Freedom is no more a necessary result of divorce than dependency is a consequence of marriage. Nonetheless, we will not deny that the Women's Movement has allowed many to leave hopeless marriages.

Deborah resented Mike's college degree, his job, his freedom and her restrictions. Despite her dissatisfactions she enjoyed her home, children and the economic security of marriage. In many ways theirs was a successful conventional marriage.

As a diversion she joined a consciousness raising group. At first both were apprehensive. Deborah didn't know how she would react, and Mike felt unsettled about his wife being with people he didn't know and ideas he considered a bit kooky. Deborah soon found her niche in the group and was supported by a receptive audience. As she ventilated her anger she began blaming Mike for keeping her dependent and unfulfilled as a person in her own right. Bewildered by her accusations, he was relieved when she finally left the group and entered college. He hoped school would be a more benign diversion which would meet her needs and get her off his back.

However, one of the things a college degree accomplished was that Deborah could now blame Mike using bigger words. Tiring of being attacked, he retaliated by coming on stronger and more authoritatively. This was exactly the proof she needed that he was the hallmark of male chauvinism. Convinced that divorcing Mike was her only path to independence and freedom, she had the divorce filed, sealed and delivered in 90 days . . . splat!

Thirty-five years young, degree in hand, Deborah entered the job market. Four futile months later she gave up searching for a mid-management position and took a job as a secretary, a position she looked down upon as common and beneath her.Angered at prospective employers who turned her down as over-qualified or inexperienced, she expounded on the cruelties of the "stupid employment system." True or not, she never stopped to evaluate whether she qualified for the position; instead, she used it as another object on which to project blame.

Despite the divorce she kept in close touch with Mike. She told him of her occupational and financial woes, followed by the usual "how-to's." In spite of her lengthy list of "if only's" and the world's inequities, Mike listened. Part of his listening was motivated by concern and another out of his anger and desire to hear her squirm, "she got hers."

Deborah's Con was, "I want to be liberated." Her ulterior message was, "You're a M.C.P. and I'll get back *at* you." His Gimmick, "I'll *let* you" belied his chauvinistic attitudes. Deborah pulled the Switch by divorcing Mike after getting what she said she needed to make her happy and liberated — a college degree.

Deborah used the Women's Movement to project blame. If anything went wrong she blamed Mike or the world for being chauvinistic or unfair. She lay waiting and pounced like a cat . . . "I got another M.C.P.!"

The sad and ironic part of their story was that neither understood what had occurred in their lives. Both had been reared in traditional homes with traditional values and had become the traditional couple. Her misunderstandings and misuse of the Women's Movement was revealed by her angry overreaction to past hurts. Rather than shift into her Adult and explore new options within the marriage, she lashed out with divorce. Baffled and angered by her change, Mike didn't search for new options either and reacted out of his traditional Parent tapes which served to reinforce Deborah's new beliefs. That Deborah continues to project blame onto Mike and the world tells us that she is still in bondage.

MONSTER BUILDING

Monster Building is a common game initiated during the separation — often continuing to the grave. Its frequency, intensity and duration depend on whether or not the grieving party has unhooked and given up his or her emotional attachment to the ex-spouse. When feelings of attachment and the separation distress have been resolved, each can look at each other realistically (in the now) without contaminating present perceptions with past hurts.

Monster Building is the practice of making a monster out of the ex in order to justify mad, bad and sad feelings. It is much like erecting a straw man upon which you can beat. Monster building also offers an opportunity to blame, and in the process absolve oneself from responsibility or guilt for the divorce.

Some examples of Monster Building are:

Mrs. Ex: "He took a trip to Vegas last week. The only trips the S.O.B. ever took me on were to Safeway!"

Mr. Ex: "The kids tell me she goes out every night. You call that a mother!"

Mrs. Ex: "He took the kids out for a good time and wound up sleeping all day. He always was a lazy slob!"

Mr. Ex: "When she goes to work and has to pay the bills, she'll know what tired really feels like. She'll even have to get out of bed before 10:00!"

Mrs. Ex: "His girlfriend loves MY stereo."

Mr. Ex: "She lets her boyfriend's dog sleep on MY favorite chair."

Mrs. Ex: "He couldn't see the kids again because he had a poker game. What a selfish, self-centered bastard he is!"

Mr. Ex: "She had another new outfit on today. You'd think she'd buy the kids something once in awhile . . . the selfish broad!"

Mrs. Ex: "He was an hour late to pick up the kids. He'll be late to his own funeral!"

Mr. Ex: "She got another speeding ticket today. She never did know where she was going . . . the dummy!"

In each instance the angry party combines present behaviors with past anger to build their case. This brutal name-calling game can be played single or multi-handed. It can be played directly with one's ex, with anyone who will listen, or alone in one's head.

Monster Building is a NOT OK energy draining position which only leads to more monsters and bad feelings. It is a nonwinning position!

MY WAY

Power games may well be the most frequently played, yet least understood of all After Divorce games. This lack of understanding rests upon the fact that the players focus on the surface conflicts of the moment and therefore miss the basic reasons for the game. In a typical "My Way" transaction, at least one of the persons maneuvers himself into a position of power in order to feel in control of his world and therefore secure. A "My Way" player is saying, "The world is capricious and unreliable and unless I'm in charge I'm vulnerable to harm." Power becomes protection.

The exercise of power occurs at three levels. The first is a direct and open demand. The second is underhanded manipulation. In both cases the players are aware of their intentions. At the third level the quest for power and control is the result of an early childhood script decision. In this instance the behavior is automatic and beneath the level of conscious awareness. Third degree players live their lives as if *each transaction* is a war maneuver with only winners and losers.

Each of us, at one time or another, has used one of these methods. While we readily admit to the first, we attempt to deny the second, and in the name of the unconscious excuse ourselves for the third. The desire for control over our own destiny is perfectly normal. However, if it is based upon a script decision which equates control with survival, the need for power can become so consuming as to encroach upon the rights and lives of others.

Wayne and Maggie have been, and still are, living with this kind of power struggle which has endured through their marriage, separation, divorce, and Maggie's remarriage. Both are potent people whose marriage was a union of passion. They were either loving or hating.

Wayne is a brilliant, self-made man who possesses tremendous ability to persuade, manipulate and control. Maggie is equally intelligent and assertive, though with Wayne she tends to hide behind the traditional female role. Despite their competitiveness, in non-personal matters such as those pertaining to business, they trust each other implicitly and are able to interact without animosity.

In their personal lives Wayne was demanding and always right. He used his Critical Parent to hook into and energize Maggie's Adapted Child. While Maggie came across to others as one you wouldn't want to tangle with, she behaved out of her Adapted Child with Wayne, attempting to get her way by manipulating with sex or money.

Their marriage boiled down to who could get whom to do what and when. While power and control were the outward manifestations of their problems, these were really defenses each used to cloak feelings of insecurity, weakness and fear of abandonment.

Following their divorce they remained in frequent contact. Some of their interactions pertained to the children, but the rest seemed motivated by the same dynamics that dominated their marriage. If Maggie was on a downer, Wayne was

Johnnie-On-The-Spot with a sympathetic ear and the power to fix things. He even went so far as to arrange blind dates and introduce her to his single friends. Maggie took the same pains to nurture him in his moments of need. Much like their marriage, things went smoothly as long as one was down and the other in a position of power and authority. However, when they were both feeling up and doing well, the power struggle ensued and the game escalated.

A year after her divorce Maggie married Dennis, an intelligent, though much less power-oriented, person than either Wayne or herself. After only a few weeks the same dynamics that had characterized her marriage to Wayne appeared in her relationship with Dennis, only this time the roles were reversed. Not only was she constantly pointing out his faults but on numerous occasions she unfavorably compared him to Wayne, telling him how much better Wayne would have handled this or that situation.

Shortly after their marriage Wayne invited Maggie and Dennis to join him and his new girlfriend at a vacation home he had recently purchased. Although she did not want to go, Maggie could not bring herself to say an open, straightforward, *unjustified no.* As she looked for a way out, she realized that any excuse she gave would have been spotted as phony; "There was no excuse I could use because he knew we had the time and money." Feeling trapped and controlled they went.

In their marriage and after divorce relationship, Wayne's Con, "Do it my way," was a cover for his need to protect himself from a world seen as harsh, unyielding and potentially dangerous. Maggie's Gimmick was her psychological corner — hating strong, dominant men, yet having no respect for weak, non-authoritative men who could neither protect, nurture nor fight with her. Either could pull the Switch by abandoning or threatening to abandon the other. Maggie's Payoff was feelings of fear, aloneness and abandonment. Wayne's was fear of being exposed for what he really was, or thought he was — unsure and vulnerable.

Despite the divorce and Maggie's remarriage, we see two assertive people maintaining the same type of personal ties they had when married. Both need each other to care for and war with.

NAIL THE COFFIN

The mere rap of the judge's gavel doesn't automatically transform our ordinary first degree game player into a destructive third degree player. Statements like, "I can't live without you," "I won't let anyone else have you," "I can't make it without you," are often made during the painful process of separation and divorce. These declarations express loss, deep sadness, aloneness and frustration.

First degree players feel them, say them and get on with life. Third degree players feel them, dwell on them and act on them. They behave from one of two life positions: "I'm OK, You're NOT OK (murder)," or, "I'm NOT OK, You're NOT OK (Suicide)." Third degree players live their lives on the edge of eternity. Their next move may be their last — or yours. Their marriages and divorces, like their lives, are punctuated with crisis as they seek out marriage partners they can intimidate, and yet who will stick around to nurse their wounds and assure them that they are OK.

A common facility of most third degree players is their uncanny ability to project blame and responsibility onto others. Their distorted perception of reality promotes their belief they are the victims of others' wrongdoings. This world view, coexistent with deep-seated feelings of NOT OKness, can, like a chemical reaction, combine and unite into a lethal explosive package. Divorce can become the catalyst!

Harry's father believed that little boys should be made of stern stuff and grow up to be strong, independent men. Although he loved Harry, he was relentless in his efforts to "grow" a strong decisive man. As a youngster Harry was never given fun spending money by his Dad and had to work when his friends were still out being little boys. His mother felt sorry for him and slipped him extra money behind his father's back. Considering the family's affluence, Harry was confused by his father's Spartan attitude and his mother's freer, less restrictive attitudes about work, fun and money. Early in life the thought was planted that men were strong and harsh and women soft and sneaky.

Seldom, if ever, did Harry get positive strokes from his

father for his efforts. The harder he worked, the more tired and non-deserving he felt. Moreover, the worse he felt, the more loving, solicitous and caring his mother became. He soon learned that the way to survive in his family was to work hard and succeed to please dad, then falter and fail to gain his mother's love and attention. This unconscious childhood decision was based on the secret (silent) messages he received from his parents' Child ego states (See Figure 5-1).

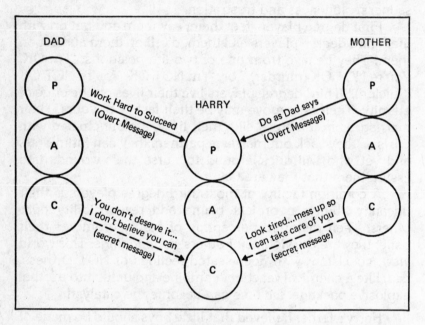

Figure 5-1
HARRY'S SCRIPT MESSAGES

Whether in business, friendship, or marriage, Harry's life pattern was the same — success followed by failure. Although he was remarkably successful and could make rapid business decisions, on the inside he was a scared little boy. The greater his success, the more he questioned whether he deserved it and if he was lovable. His childhood script decision led to a series of counter-productive moves designed to short-circuit success in order to get someone to show him love and affection.

Harry's choice of a wife fit his script perfectly. Marge's traditional upbringing placed success and status, through marriage, high on her priority list. She saw Harry as having all the ingredients necessary to reach her goal and worked hard as the woman behind the man. When he began his downward spiral she knew, just like his mother, when, where and how to apply the bandages. Unfortunately, she bit off more than she could chew!

Harry's inability to sustain success left their personal, financial and marital lives in a constant state of real or impending turmoil. In an attempt to block out persistent feelings of NOT OKness, (he didn't believe he deserved his wins) he began drinking heavily. His drinking soon reached alcoholic proportions.

Over the next eight years Marge vacillated between behaving like a mother with a sick infant and persecuting like a bitch. Her behavior was a re-creation of Harry's childhood — at times she behaved like his father and at others like his mother. The game escalated to the third degree level when he became physically abusive, was jailed for public drunkenness, and hospitalized for injuries sustained during barroom brawls.

Marge held onto her wish that they could accomplish great things together and continued to bandage his wounds while lecturing, threatening and waiting for the next go-round. Harry then dipped deeply into his third degree game bag by making several suicide attempts. Although Marge knew he was serious, his friends and relatives passed it off as just another of Harry's irresponsible drunken stunts — "After all, drunks sometimes wreck their cars or take too many sleeping pills."

Physically and emotionally exhausted, she began questioning and searching. With the urging and support of a friend, Marge joined a therapy group. Six months later her world made more sense, and with her strength revitalized she filed for divorce. Harry's response was catastrophic! He screamed, begged and threatened suicide. Her resolve weakened by his suicidal threats and promises he would change, she took the Con and stopped the divorce proceedings.

Harry's script was more powerful than his promises! Within six months he pulled the Switch and was behaving exactly as before. With a year of therapy now behind her, Marge understood how their scripts intertwined and the reasons and ways they were poisonous to each other. She also learned that she had at least three options available to her:

1. Remain in the marriage and be a willing game partner.

2. Leave the marriage cleanly and without guilt, knowing that remaining together, without significant change, reinforced the negative aspects of each's script.

3. Divorce with the fear that if he committed suicide she would be responsible.

Marge chose the second option. Harry responded by pulling a third degree Switch and made a suicide attempt, which for five days left him on the brink of death. As he lay in the intensive care unit, she momentarily weakened. She asked herself:

1. Was she responsible? Had she *pounded the nails into his coffin?*

2. What responsibility would her children and family lay at her feet?

3. Was she going to be seen as cruel and uncaring?

4. Would she and her children be stigmatized if he died by his own hand?

5. If he lived and she went back, could she survive that hell?

With the aid of her therapist she saw Harry's suicide attempts for what they really were — blackmail! She understood that leaving him was her only viable choice, for to remain in the marriage was tantamount to nailing *both* their coffins shut.

Harry pulled through. Frightened for them both, she proceeded with the divorce. Although Harry is still flirting with disaster, he has taken some positive steps in his own behalf. While the chances of another suicide attempt remain, Marge no longer feels responsible for Harry. As a result he is beginning to enjoy and assume responsibility for his successes.

In a third degree game such as this, therapy is essential. Left to their own devices, third degree game players set themselves up for the courtroom, the hospital or the morgue.

HOW'S YOUR BLOOD PRESSURE?

Recent research supports the contention that people can and do die of broken hearts. If you just divorced you probably know what we mean as you listen to your favorite sad song, feel weakened by that 20 pounds you lost, and look at that ashtray filled with the remnants of your nervous tension. Stories about elderly widows and widowers rapidly following their spouses to death are also common.

At this time when we are most in need of other caring people, many of us withdraw into cocoons of isolation and self-pity. Even those who throw themselves into work or social activities can do so without really *being with another.* While they may be *next to* or *alongside of,* they may never touch another's vital center.

Dr. James Lynch of the University of Maryland Medical School has made a study of and written a book on the "broken heart phenomenon."[1] His work is a shocking testimony to the physical trauma of loneliness. Dr. Lynch believes that the loss of love and companionship is a leading cause of chronic illness and premature death.

Although the concept of stress as a contributor to heart and other diseases is generally accepted, the idea that lack of companionship can have similar results is only now being seriously considered. In his work with patients suffering from a wide variety of illnesses such as migraines, high blood pressure and cancer, he became convinced of the power of love and the destructive potential of loneliness. Dr. Lynch warns that a society in which the rate of divorce is rising, the family fragmenting, where social and community ties are transient, and where children and the aged are neglected, our physical survival is threatened.

In each of the three years, 1975-1978, over *one million* marriages ended in divorce. Between 1965 and 1975 the number of single parent households nearly doubled from 2.7

---

[1] James J. Lynch, *The Broken Heart,* Basic Books, Inc., New York, 1977.

to 5 million. Examination of mortality statistics revealed that life styles which promoted loneliness were highly correlated with increased incidence of physical illness. Regardless of age, sex or race, those who lived alone had death rates two to ten times higher than those of married couples. For example, divorced white women between the ages of 15 and 65 had a cervical cancer death rate about 2½ times as great as that of their married counterparts. Comparable figures, for men and women alike, can be found for nearly every major cause of death.[2]

Since how we feel is related to how we live, stable, satisfying relationships tend to reduce such self-destructive behaviors as drinking, smoking and overeating. Dr. Lynch suggests that those who lack or lose the comfort of another caring person may be deprived of nature's most potent antidote to stress . . . love and nurturance.

If you are divorced or widowed, have isolated yourself and are concentrating on your pain and loneliness, then there is all the more reason to understand the physical consequences of your behavior. The old saw, "I never want to get involved again because I don't want to be vulnerable," is just that . . . an instrument to hack away at your physical and emotional health.

At the other end of the spectrum is the "Have Orgasm Will Travel" player who embarks on a binge of hedonistic pleasure as a way to remain distant and uninvolved. Intimacy is risky, but where is the joy in loneliness, self-pity or sporting sex?

"How's Your Blood Pressure?" is an example of how one's health can be used to initiate a game. The initiator can be either the ailing or non-ailing party. As with other games the surface issue — health — is not the real reason; rather, it is a mechanism to establish contact in order to start a game.

The initiator of a health game uses one of the three basic Cons:

1. Without me you got sick.
2. You need me to take care of you.
3. If I get sick enough you'll come back to me.

---

[2]Ibid., pg. 9.

Della was stunned when Nat announced that he was leaving her for another woman. During the early phase of the divorce adjustment period, her misery was enhanced by Nat's happiness with his new love. Over the next eleven months she reassembled her disjointed and bent parts. During this same period Nat's new relationship went on the proverbial rocks.

They lived in the same neighborhood and frequently ran into each other. When they met they usually touched base and shared what was happening in each other's lives. It never failed that during the conversation Della inquired about Nat's blood pressure. When they parted Nat always felt let down and later that day had one of his high blood pressure headaches. It took a half dozen or so of these conversations and a meeting with his therapist before he realized that Della, like his parents, was stroking him for his illness. Her apparent concern over his health and well-being was actually a Con. He took the bait and listened out of his need to be cared for and nurtured (Gimmick?). The game came to a screeching halt when upon their next meeting Nat stopped only long enough for a brief but courteous hello and goodbye. No high blood pressure strokes — no symptoms!

A related version of "How's Your Blood Pressure?" occurs when the well party inquires about the other's ailment in the secret hopes that he is not doing well. The message underlying the Con is, "When we were married I took care of you and now look what you've done to yourself. You can't get along without me." Much like the first version, the idea is to throw out an emotional re-hooker and when the bait is taken, pull the Switch by backing off and leaving the other alone and sickly.

The third version of the game is played similarly, but for a different purpose. Rather than attempt to inflict additional pain, the initiator throws out re-hookers in an attempt to forge a reconciliation. The ulterior message is, "You need me to take care of you."

In the fourth version the game is initiated by the ailing party. In this instance he permits himself to become ill or lets an existing illness become worse. The intent is to produce enough guilt in the ex-spouse in the hope that he will return to the relationship.

You couldn't change him while you were married, so you're sure as hell not going to change him after the divorce! You've lived with him long enough to know the scoop. Look back over your lives. Your marital history will give you all the information you need to predict his behavior. Even if you are only an average estimator, by using your predictive skills you can stop frustrating yourself because — he wouldn't, he does, he says but won't . . . Holding onto false expectations and the wish that he'll be different is gamey.

Once you accept the fact that he is he, you are you, and neither can *make* the other different, you are open to new and positive options for yourself and the After Divorce relationship. Caution: If you give up your After Divorce games, be prepared, at least in the beginning, to feel an emptiness, a void. Your After Divorce games filled and structured your time. You will now have to plug the void with positive transactions.

Successful After Divorce relationships consist of four basic elements:

1. Courtesy,
2. Financial Commitment,
3. Parental Commitment, and
4. Minimal Personal Contact.

Courtesy means treating your ex as *you* would like to be treated. Cut the barbs, attacks, put downs and getting back ats. Another aspect of courtesy is keeping the other abreast of significant happenings in the children's lives . . . from illness to winning a ribbon at field day. If talking won't work, write a note.

Commitments to financial and parental responsibilities are straightforward. Do what you're committed to do. If your visitation agreement says Saturday at 9:00 a.m., be there Saturday at 9:00 a.m. If the support check is due the First — have it there the First. If you tell little Paul you'll take him or do with him, then take or do.

Grant/Berke's Theory of After Divorce Relationships is $C = H^2$, or the greater the contact the higher the probability for hassle. Positive interaction hinges on the divorced couple being emotionally unhooked and available for honest, game free transactions.

YOU'LL BE SORRY WHEN I DIE

**EENY, MEENY, MINY, MO,
TO WHICH PARENT SHOULD I GO?
IF I HOLLER, WHO WILL PAY,
BY THE HOUR OR THE DAY?**

"Until now I didn't realize how much my children and I missed the boat with each other during my divorce. It was as if we experienced the same events and yet were a million miles apart."

... A mother after a talk with her teenagers.

"Sometimes I have the feeling I don't count or even exist. I am seldom remembered on my birthday or Father's Day. It's like I am Mr. Money Bags yet they see their mother, not me, as supporting them. I wonder if she's turning the kids against me?"

... A father of three preteens.

During the emotional upheaval of separation and divorce, each family member tends to withdraw and focus on himself. Each looks out onto his rapidly changing and uncertain world through his own little peephole. The peephole, developed out of a need for self-protection and survival, results in distorted perceptions, since important information is blocked off from Adult consideration. Mom, dad and the kids live the same events, but see and experience them differently.

CHILDREN AND SEPARATION

You can estimate the size of your children's peepholes, and the extent of their distortions by asking yourself the following questions.

1. Did you explain, in language they understood, what was happening to their family and what the outcome would be?
2. Were they assured that they are loved and will not be abandoned by either parent?
3. Were they assured that they were not the cause of the divorce?
4. Do they understand that divorce is between parents and not between parents and their children?
5. Was visitation openly discussed and did they have any say about the arrangements?
6. Were they invited to share their feelings, thoughts and questions about the divorce?
7. Did they see, hear or participate in parental conflicts? If so, did they take sides?
8. Have you invited a conflict of loyalties by talking to them about that S.O.B., their other parent?

The less children understand and the more that is left to their imaginations, the greater will be their distortions. To keep their perspective (peepholes) as wide as possible, these tips suggested by Dr. Robert S. Weiss can help.

1. All children react to separation and divorce with fear and anxiety. Give them abundant supplies of love and affection.
2. Children, even the very young, need to be kept informed. However, do not overload them with information they cannot comprehend.
3. Children do better if the non-custody parent continues to parent.
4. A child's most important source of security is a confident parent as head of the household.

5. Fathers without custody can contribute to their children's growth and development by supporting their ex-wife. The less burdened she is by conflict with him, the more energy she will have for herself and the children.

6. The less changed in other areas of the child's life the better, i.e., home, school, church, friends, etc.

7. Children should be permitted to develop and mature at their own pace. Do not overprotect or encourage little Johnny to be the "Little Man" of the house or little Susie to be "Miniature Mommy."

8. Establish a happy, rewarding life of your own. Unless both parents feel good about themselves, particularly the custody parent, they cannot help but project their bad feelings onto the children.[1]

Children, even those under two, identify with and feel connected to both parents. When mother and father separate they feel divided and disconnected. Separation and "after divorce warfare" make matters worse, as they can lead to a child taking sides. Since both parents are part of him, if he sides against one, he is, in effect, siding against part of himself.

This can be a double negative — rejection of part of self and a conflict of parental loyalties. Depression, withdrawal, regression to an earlier stage of development, physical symptoms, and aggressive acting out are likely to result. Parents can prevent this kind of internal strife and its behavioral consequences by supporting each other as parents and people.

If in the early phase of the separation your children are not sharing their thoughts and feelings and seem to be taking things very much in stride, consider this a possible red alert. They may be stockpiling feelings. The following thoughts, feelings and questions are to be expected.

They feel scared, "What will happen to me?" They feel guilty, "Did I cause Mom and Dad to divorce?" They feel angry, "If I'm not to blame why is this happening to me?"

[1]Robert S. Weiss, *Marital Separation,* Basic Books, 1975, pgs. 227-232.

They feel powerless, "Why don't I have a say about this?" They feel sad, "I'm losing Dad, our house and my friends." They feel embarrassed, "What will my friends say?" They feel conflicted, "If I love Mom, can I still love Dad?" They feel confused, "What next?"

The Manner In Which They Are Told

If possible, tell the children jointly and in an atmosphere of mutual love and concern for their well-being. The presence of both parents offers a sense of security and decreases the likelihood of one parent coming off as the villain.

Tell them a week or two before the actual separation. This will give them time to digest the news, ask some of their questions and begin the process of working through their feelings. Telling them just before the separation leaves them no time to adjust and tends to increase feelings of abandonment and mistrust. Too much advance notice may stimulate or heighten reconciliation fantasies.

The best approach is openness and honesty. When they ask the inevitable whys, tell them, but in a way which fits their ages and ability to comprehend. If they are widely spaced in age, schedule some time alone with each so you can tailor the explanation to fit their levels of maturity.

Honesty helps to stabilize a youngster's trust in his parents at a time when it is most needed. An open, straightforward approach provides children with a model of two people who, despite serious conflict, are willing and able to work together toward the solution of a difficult and emotionally charged problem. While honesty is valued, you needn't share intimate details. This role model will serve them well in later life.

Age at the Time of Divorce

Most children, regardless of age, take divorce hard. While there seem to be differences in the impact of divorce as it relates to age, research in this area is still mixed and the findings are inconclusive.

Siblings

The presence of brothers and sisters may influence a child's reaction to divorce. The data is only beginning to take shape. It appears that having a sibling of nearly the same age helps as children bond together forming their own support system. However, if the children are widely spaced, the eldest may take on too much responsibility for younger siblings and attempt to become a surrogate parent.

Visitation with the Non-Custody Parent

Free and open access to the non-custody parent is in a child's best interest. Seldom is this possible. The next best option is shared or joint custody. In this arrangement the child shares his time, as equally as possible, with both parents — i.e., seasonally, according to school semesters, or during long vacation periods. Unless both parents reside in the same school district and are willing and able to engage in the amount of contact necessary to make this arrangement work, this is not a viable option.

Frequent contact on a routine, though not inflexible, basis is the most workable option. Consistent contact with the non-custody parent helps a youngster develop a sense of security about the "away" parent as well as a sense of his own lovability. A child whose non-custody parent deserts him often interprets this as a negative indication of his own self-worth.

It is imperative that the custodial parent not use visitation as a means to control the children. If the custody parent shows disappointment, fear, or sadness when the child leaves to visit the other parent, this may stimulate guilt in the child, which may evolve into feelings of divided loyalties.

Our reply to a divorced father's letter illustrates the impact of the non-custodial parent.

> California psychologist Joan Kelly found that no matter how frequently a divorced father sees his children, they complain that they don't see him enough. Their intense wish to see him more often seems tied to a denial of the divorce and a preoccupation with reconciliation fantasies. Dr. Kelly found that young children tend to grieve openly for their absent father, while children over nine tend to express their grief through anger.[2]

---

[2]Joan Kelly, Address to the American Psychological Assoc., Sept., 1978.

Dr. Ross Parke, a University of Illinois psychologist, warned against believing that fathers lack the capacity and ability to nurture their infant children. He reported that several studies have demonstrated that middle and lower class fathers were just as nurturing as mothers. They touched, looked at, kissed and talked to their newborns as much as mothers, and rocked and held them more.

Although fathers were less available to feed and diaper their children, the studies indicated that they played with their babies more often than mothers. At age two, toddlers preferred their fathers as playmates.[3]

See him as often as possible.

Remarriage

A child's grief over his parents' divorce may be protracted, delayed, or even avoided. Working through and resolving divorce-related stress may take some children several years. Since the average time between divorce and remarriage is three years, a child may still be working through the loss of the original family unit when a parent remarries. Therefore, a youngster's involvement with his own grief may impede adjustment to the reconstituted family.

To a child in this situation, relating to two parents of the same sex may represent or intensify a conflict of loyalties. A child may believe that by accepting the stepparent he is rejecting the biological parent. Even more frightening is the question of whether or not he will lose the love of his natural parent if the stepparent is accepted. The presence of a stepparent during this critical period can also enhance the reality of his loss, i.e., another is here to take Dad's/Mom's place.

Unless these issues are anticipated and understood they may provide additional grist for the game mill. If you are going to remarry, tell your children you are doing so to meet needs which can only be satisfied by another adult, and while you want them to like and eventually love your new spouse, your only demand is for courtesy and respect. Assure them a stepparent is not a replacement for a biological parent.

[3]*Marriage And Divorce Today*, Vol. 3, No. 5, Sept. 18, 1978, Pg. 4.

FATHERS AND SEPARATION

Until recently our culture has demanded that women be dependent upon yet care for and nurture men. Men, in turn, were relegated to the world of work in order to support *their* woman and children. The result of this cultural mandate is that most men over thirty are unskilled, ignorant, don't wish to, or refuse to attend to the mundane yet necessary tasks of daily living. Some consider these endeavors a demeaning intrusion on life's purpose — real work.

I, Mel Berke, am a case in point. Although I had set this day aside to write, I found it necessary to tackle several household chores before I could get to my desk. I resented these intrusions on my "real" calling. However, I didn't resent the intrusions on this very same time posed by several calls from patients. These interruptions were seen as an affirmation of my value and worth.

This statement from a man who believes in the concept of personal independence and liberation is telling. Imagine the resentment, frustration and anger a *full fledged* M.C.P. might feel!

For a man, divorce means that the foundation upon which his conceptions of home, manhood, fatherhood, and the purpose for which he labors, has shifted to a new and uncertain base. Those aspects of his life he once looked upon as givens no longer exist. He must learn to do what he once expected from his wife, plus create a new life style, which includes single parenting. For the newly separated and long time married man, this is a monumental and frightening task.

A further issue a divorcing man may now legitimately consider is the question of custody. Until recently, few men sought and even fewer were awarded custody. For the most part, they and society considered women better able and more *naturally* suited to care for children. Despite the fact that most men have little training and experience in child rearing, with few exceptions there is no reason to believe that women can do a better job. The question of custody should rest on desire and rational considerations as opposed to outmoded cultural tapes and legal precedents.

Most men still become "part-time fathers," and they must learn to nurture, discipline, play and leave their mark under a new and different set of circumstances. Their job is made all the more difficult because of the time constraint, i.e., every other weekend and vacations. You just don't divorce on Monday and by Saturday have developed a satisfying method of parenting. What worked one month after the separation will alter with changes in experience, life style and circumstances. It takes time for a couple to develop their particular parenting style. Why should it be any different for a single person? This awareness may short-circuit some conflicts between ex-spouses as each comes to realize the time and effort it takes to learn how to be a single parent.

Visitation is an *artifact* of divorce. It is an artificial and contrived way of relating to children. This is not to say it can't be a fun and intimate time of sharing. However, in the beginning it is a time of experimentation, oftentimes resulting in more stress and conflict than pleasure. For these reasons the adults should be patient and forego fault-finding in order to justify negative feelings toward one another. The better a father feels about his parenting skills and the quality of his relationship with his children, the less likelihood there is of negative strokes and game transactions.

The artificiality of visitation is highlighted when a father and his children must say goodby at the end of each visit. The potential for sadness and the rekindling of feelings of abandonment are multifold. For these reasons children frequently return to their mothers upset, whining and difficult to live with. Misunderstanding the psychodynamics of the situation and attributing their misbehavior to a bad visit or spoiling, some mothers complain, "After only two days he's turned them into brats. He is spoiling the hell out of them." An awareness of this process enables a mother to help her children work through their feelings by encouraging them to talk, i.e., "I understand you're upset because you love and had to leave Dad."

After a super visit some children instigate a conflict with Dad just before they have to leave. By doing so a youngster may be helping his Father say goodby simply because it is easier to say goodby when you are angry then when you are feeling warm and close. Once again, the most beneficial way of dealing with this situation is to encourage the child to verbalize his feelings.

A further issue loaded with game possibilities is differences in parental values. Most parents want and believe they have the right to shape the values and attitudes of their children. However, the non-custodial parent must face the fact that he or she must forego considerable influence on the lives of his children. If the non-custodial parent, typically the father, does not accept the fact his children must live according to the rules, values, and philosophies of his ex-wife, the adults will be at war and the children will be the victims.

This should not be interpreted to mean that a father must not teach his values or establish his own set of rules. The crucial issue is that he should not promote a conflict of loyalties in his children. It is perfectly appropriate for a father to say, "I know in your house you do it that way, but here we do it this way." Children do learn to adapt to the realities of their surroundings. A custodial mother can lessen the potential for conflicted loyalties by accepting that her ex-husband may be exposing the children to values and ideas with which she disagrees.

Parents who war over whom and what Johnny should be like never really end their marriage as they bicker about those very differences in values and attitudes which led to the divorce in the first place.

MOTHERS AND SEPARATION

The single most important thing a newly separated mother with custody can do for her children is to create a happy and rewarding *life of her own*. As long as she maintains herself in a frightened, angry, resentful place, she will be a liability to herself and her children.

Easier said than done, but imperative! A newly separated mother is struggling to establish her own personal, social and financial identity while dealing with the daily tasks of parenting, housekeeping and career. If she is the custody parent, she has no choice but to get her parenting act together quickly. While her personal reaction to the divorce may last from one to three years, the reconstruction of her familial life must occur within weeks.

When a mother separates from her husband, fear, anger and resentment can become her staff of life. If she feeds off these feelings, she will view herself as powerless. At this crucial point her primary tie to stability, and possibly even contact with her husband, is the children. The inherent danger of this position is that she may unconsciously become dependent upon her children to meet all her needs for closeness, affiliation and comfort. Since children cannot completely fulfill these needs, resentment and disillusionment are nearly always the result. It is at this point that she and her children are most vulnerable to games.

If she holds onto her anger at her ex-husband, she may use the children as a way to get back at him. This is a frequent occurrence even among rational, loving mothers who, at the conscious level, would shirk at the thought of using their children as pawns. Nonetheless, during this period of crisis and turmoil, thinking becomes distorted. The solution is to unhook from her ex-husband and establish an independent identity and life of her own.

Women should give themselves permission to decide rationally whether or not they wish to be the custody parent. Inasmuch as society demands a woman seek custody or be labeled as "unfit" or "unnatural," many women seek or accept custody to avoid ridicule. Others become the custody parent by *default.*

The following letter and our reply speak to this issue.

Q. "I recently filed for divorce and my family and friends are shocked because I think my husband should have custody of the kids. I love my children and am not a bad mother, but believe that their father would be the better custodial parent. It's not that I'm unfit, but his relationship with them is better than mine. After all the criticism I've taken, I wonder if I'm wrong and should change my mind?"

A: "You are a gutsy mother! It takes wisdom and courage to assess your parental skills and those of your husband and make the choice that is best for your children. Motherhood doesn't qualify one as the better parent anymore than fatherhood makes for a less adequate parent.

The number of mothers who do not want custody is rising. While most mothers do not express this thought publicly, in the privacy of the consultation office this has become an increasingly frequent statement. Since our culture tends to revere motherhood, a woman who does not seek custody is often ridiculed. The same attitude has made it more acceptable for fathers to shun custody. Custody should be sought and granted in light of what's best for the children. In a landmark State Supreme Court decision, Dr. Lee Salk, author and psychologist, won custody of his two children. Neither parent attempted to prove the other unfit. The pivotal issue was the children's best interest.

If you have evaluated the situation clearly, and are sure of your position, act on it. In doing so, you are demonstrating your love."

The following two chapters will not touch upon all or even the majority of game transactions between children and their divorced parents. That task would take a volume in itself. Our purpose is to highlight some of the more visible and potent generators of conflict which can lead to games. This chapter will focus on games initiated by children.

YOU'LL BE SORRY WHEN I DIE

Gabe plunked all sixty pounds of himself down on the front porch steps, and bit his lip to keep from crying. If he cried he just knew someone would come out and say, "Gabe, don't be a crybaby!" Since his Mom and Dad had divorced, it seemed like someone was always telling him, "Gabe, empty the garbage . . . Gabe, go out and play . . . Gabe, we're talking . . . Gabe, go to bed." He thought about his brother and two sisters. "Big deal teenagers. You'd think they'd figure out an eight-year-old knows something."

He picked up a rock and threw it so it would skip across the street, sort of like when he and his Dad went fishing and they skipped rocks across the water. He wondered if he'd ever get to do that again. "Gosh, I hate *now,*" Gabe muttered as he looked down at the hole in his sneaker and pushed his big toe through it. "Mom works, Dad's gone, and those big deal yak yaks in the house boss me around like I'm a nobody. That's what I am, a *nobody* since Dad left," he thought as he angrily threw another rock, almost hitting a car. "Boy, if I died then they'd be sorry."

When his parents separated, the entire family tried to protect Gabe. Although he overheard bits and pieces of conversations and watched with little boy eyes, no one ever told him what was happening to his family, why his Dad left, and what would happen to him. His family didn't mean to hurt him, but bigger people's actions based on bigger people's perceptions left him confused, left out, scared and angry. As his fright and insecurity mounted, the quieter and less expressive he became.

Over the next few months Gabe's behavior became intolerable. He would agree to do something and then quietly go about his business as if he had never been asked. A simple, "Wash your hands before dinner," invariably turned into a hassle as Gabe showed up at the table with dirty hands. This passive-aggressive behavior was the only way Gabe could get back AT. He didn't do anything bad, he just didn't do. In his way he got to them as they worked harder and harder, while he did less and less.

Taking a page out of a behavior modification book, his Mother posted rules, regulations and consequences on the refrigerator door. "Gabe was going to learn to be more responsible!" she said. The harder everyone pushed and the greater the consequences, the more depressed Gabe felt and the more infantile his behavior became.

Because he kept his feelings locked up inside and had no means of expressing them other than through quiet defiance, he began thinking about ways to get back at his family. He fantasized his death, the funeral and the guilt and sadness his family would surely feel. While transient thoughts about death, as a way to express anger and get revenge, are normal types of childhood behavior, in Gabe's case the thoughts became obsessive. He began asking his parents questions like, "If I fell out of the treehouse would I die?" and, "If I died what would you do with my bike?" Death fantasies became part of his dream world and he began having nightmares.

Concerned, his parents consulted a child psychologist. They learned that Gabe's death fantasies were his way of expressing stored up anger at his family — "You left me so I'll leave you." After several family therapy sessions, which included his father, he felt the parental permission he needed to express his feelings, ask his questions and receive his answers. When he again felt part of the family, his negativism and death fantasies vanished.

I'LL GO LIVE WITH DAD

Sara's face appeared pale and tense as she stared down at her nine-year-old son, Billy. She had told him to clean his room and he shot back in a nasty threatening tone, "I don't have to, and if you make me, I'll go live with Dad!"

Sara short-circuited. Had she spent most of the month supporting and mothering a child whose Father had recently moved out only to be threatened by a three-foot replica of her husband? The anger and exhaustion welled up inside her. She exploded: "All right, pack your things and call your Father to pick you up!"

Because she responded out of anger and didn't really mean what she said, guilt and self-recrimination quickly followed. Several hours and one dirty room later Sara apologized. The result of this transaction was indelibly printed upon Billy's young personality. He learned how powerful his threats were.

Sara spent the following months attempting to prove what a good mother she was so that Billy wouldn't leave her. Billy had learned to control his Mother with those five magic words, "I'll go live with Dad." The "clean your room" episode spread into so many other areas of their lives that living with him became intolerable. He learned his lesson well and played his blackmail game whenever the opportunity presented itself.

Had Sara's positive stroke reserve not been so depleted, she could have checked her anger, shifted into her Adult and figured out that this was Billy's way of testing her. Instead, she responded out of rejection and anger from her Child ego state. Billy's test was simple: "Daddy left me, will you? How do I know you really want me?"

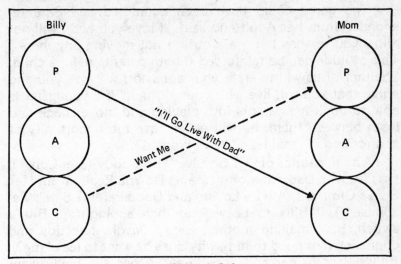

Figure 6-1

Figure 6-1 illustrates the overt message from Billy's Critical Parent to his Mother's Child ego state and the secret message from his Child to his Mother's Nurturing Parent ego state.

Figure 6-2 shows the overt transaction from Sara's Critical Parent to Billy's Child ego state and the unspoken Child to Child message of hurt and rejection.

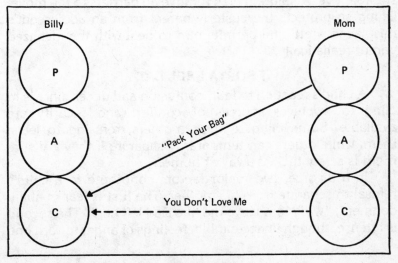

Figure 6-2

The game could have been countered had Sara responded from her Adult and said, "I love you and I will not allow you to threaten me. You are not moving anywhere." This attitude can be reinforced if both parents tell the child, "Neither of us will tolerate your behavior. We love you and agree that you will live with your Mother." If a youngster is able to hook his parents into playing and moves back and forth between them, he will never have the opportunity of confronting his real fear, "Am I Wanted?"

The dynamics of "I'll Go Live With Daddy" are: Con, I'll Go Live with Dad; Ulterior message, Do You Really Want Me? Sara's Gimmick, Am I a Loving and Good Parent? Sara's Response, Tell Billy to Leave and then apologizing; Billy's switch, Blackmailing mother; Sara's Payoff, rejection and confusion (I'm good to him, why does he want to leave me?); Billy's Payoff, fear and uncertainty, (Does she really want me?).

A related version of "I'll Go Live With Dad" occurs when a teenager believes that his happiness lies in living with the non-custody parent who, unbeknownst to him, does not wish the responsibility of full-time parenthood. In an attempt to shield the child from the truth, the custody parent blocks the move. This tactic reinforces the adolescent's belief that the custody parent is indeed an ogre, thereby intensifying his desire to move. A solution is to remove all barriers to the move. Doing so protects the custody parent from an adolescent's misplaced wrath and permits him to deal with the idealized parent realistically.

I SORTA FEEL BAD

A child's reaction to fear, confusion and uncertainty is to cling to whatever sources of comfort and security are available. Some cling to their mothers, refusing to leave them, while others can temporarily separate if they are sure mom is safely tucked away at home.

In a divorce, two major factors contribute to a child's refusal to separate from his mother. The first is fear of abandonment, "Will Mom leave me like Dad left her?" The second is intense, though unacceptable, feelings of anger toward one or both parents for putting him in this frightening position. The unacceptability of these feelings results from the fact that young children tend to confuse hostile, destructive and even murderous feelings with actual behavior. For them, feeling is akin to doing. Most often these feelings are unconscious. Therefore, children place themselves in the paradoxical position of remaining at a parent's side in order to protect the parents from their (the children's) own unconscious impulses.

When Buster was five years old, his father died in Vietnam. While he had little conscious memory of him, he remembered how good it felt to be held and played with by a Daddy. His Mother remarried when he was seven, and he was overjoyed about having a father. When his Mother divorced, three years later, he felt his world had come apart. He was scared, angry and couldn't understand why he lost another Daddy.

Several days after the separation, while dressing for school, he began feeling sick. The closer the time came to leave for school, the sicker he felt. Feeling guilty for what she had done (taking away his father), his mother stayed home from work and gave Buster *extra* large doses of loving. Over the next three weeks Buster experienced several more "attacks," and each time his mother overreacted. Buster's unconscious soon picked up the message that the royal road to attention, control over Mom, and no school was illness.

Within weeks, feelings of loss and abandonment were unconsciously utilized to initiate a blackmail/avoidance game. Whenever he wished to avoid a situation or task, an upset stomach and a "I Sorta Feel Bad" sent Mom into an oversolicitous, infantilizing tizzy. Feeling ill, originally based on genuine feelings of fright and loss, was transformed into an avoidance-control game. Had his mother not felt so guilty and overreacted, his symptoms could have been appropriately dealt with and the game avoided.

If you are into a game of "I Sorta Feel Bad" and your child won't go to school, to camp, or to . . . try these simple and effective measures.

1. Unless he has a fever, red throat, spots all over his body or an illness confirmed by your doctor, he goes.

2. Take him even if he screams, yells bloody murder and creates holy hell. Don't feel ashamed or embarrassed if you have to physically take him into the school building. Teachers and principals have seen and dealt with this type of behavior before.

3. If he becomes "ill" at school and the nurse can find nothing physically wrong, he stays. A few boring hours alone in the nurse's office can be a wonder drug.

4. If his behavior persists three weeks or longer, consult your family doctor. If a physical cause cannot be found ask for a referral to a child therapist.

"I Sorta Feel Bad" can also be the result of a child's conscious or unconscious wish to reunite his parents. Illness can be used as a mechanism to put parents in contact with each other in order to work on a common problem — him. The hope is that togetherness will promote a reconciliation.

TOMMY TROUBLE

Six weeks before his parents separated, Tommy's behavior at school became provocative and aggressive. He challenged his teachers, didn't do his class work, and vacillated between being the class clown and the class bully. His behavior in the neighborhood was just as bad. He went around with a chip on his shoulder and always had to be first. Shortly after the separation his Mother began receiving complaints from other mothers and calls from the school.

Teacher conferences, talks with other mothers and her own observations led to the conclusion that Tommy wished to get caught. It also became apparent that his motivation was not to hurt others as much as it was to call attention to himself. The reasons for this kind of behavior are multifold and range from anger and depression to feelings of guilt over causing the divorce. In Tommy's case reconciliation fantasies were the motivating force. If he could create havoc and get into enough trouble, his parents would have to see each other in order to deal with the problem — him.

Tommy's Con was to behave badly. His secret message was, "I want you back together." The Gimmick he was attempting to hook was his parents' love and concern for him and *feelings of guilt.* Their Response to his Con will determine if the initiation escalates into a full-fledged game.

Should his parents reconcile for Tommy's sake, they will have taken the bait. Because they have not resolved their differences, additional conflict will inevitably erupt and Tommy will again have to intercede the only way he knows, by acting out.

Parents who make it clear that they will not reconcile, despite a child's misbehavior, will lessen the probability if not completely avoid this game. If the child's behavior persists, consult a therapist.

PING PONG

Betty and Jerry divorced and agreed to let Brett, age 13, decide with whom he wanted to live. Brett chose to live with his Mother. Since Jerry's business necessitated a move to the West Coast, it was decided that Brett would visit him during holidays and school vacations.

After their lengthy time apart, Father and son were anxious to see each other and Jerry entertained Brett royally. Disneyland, motion picture studio tours, and the California beaches were a blast. Brett returned home after the Christmas holidays bragging about his Father, their good times and his wish to spend more time with him. Brett's comments hooked Betty and she began feeling competitive with Jerry and resentful of Brett. Her ambivalent feelings toward Brett (love and anger over his idealized and distorted view of Jerry) resulted in her becoming more permissive, as if to woo Brett over to her side. As a result Brett became increasingly demanding and a discipline problem. When she finally put her foot down, Brett yelled foul and made noises about going to live with his father.

Just before leaving to spend the summer with his Father, it was decided that Brett would remain with him for the entire year. In the beginning Father and son picked up where they left off. After several weeks of playing host and entertainer, Jerry realized that he couldn't continue living his life as a tour guide and set rules and limits. By mid-summer Brett was dis-illusioned over having to live under the same, if not tighter, controls than he had with his Mother. The circle was com-pleted when, at summer's end, he begged to go back to his Mother. Because of the conflicts between them Jerry re-lented. Brett remained with his Mother for the entire school year, but as he neared 15, thoughts of California beaches, bi-kini clad "chicks" and the car his Father had promised to buy him dominated his fantasies. The thoughts of a car parked in the carport just awaiting his return began eating away at him. The outcome was predictable — one hellish time for both Mother and son.

This multi-handed game resulted in three monsters. Two parents competing with each other for their son and one self-centered fifteen-year-old who couldn't get along unless he got his way.

Betty and Jerry's first error was to leave the decision where Brett would live up to him. While they should have taken Brett's wishes into consideration, he should not have been left in control of the final decision. Their second mistake was to let Brett's comments hook their feelings to the degree that they became competitive. The third error was to permit Brett to bounce back and forth between them. While deci-sions about custody and living arrangements should not be rigid, by the same token, they should be made with an eye toward stability.

Giving Brett the choice of with whom he would live placed him in a corner. Having the power to choose one parent over the other led to feelings of divided loyalties. Leav-ing one parent for the other was a test to see whether either cared enough to take a firm stand and remove him from his corner. Each failed the test.

YOU SPENT MY CHILD SUPPORT

If there is a list of "for sures" in divorce, one of the "for surest" is conflict over money. Money games do not begin and end with adults. Children can also be hard money game players. However the remarks and behaviors of some chil-dren, which appear to be game initiations, are often the result of naiveté about money matters. These naive comments can escalate into full-fledged money games if parents tug on an unintentional hook out of their own hang-ups. However, some youngsters throw out true Cons designed to hook into a parent's Gimmick.

Eight-year-old Jan knew that her Daddy loved her, and that one of the ways he showed it was by sending money. Since the money was supposed to be for her, sort of like an allowance, she wondered why she never got to see it. When she asked her Mother she always got the same answer, "Your Father sends the child support to me and I use it to buy you things." Jan accepted her Mother's explanation without fully understanding what she had been told.

During the first year of her parents' divorce, she often asked her Mother to buy her some of those neat toys and games she saw advertised on television. More often than not her Mother replied, "We don't have the money." Since her Father sent her Mom money to buy her things she didn't understand the "No's" and became silently angry.

Adding to her confusion were her observations of her Mother gearing up for a new life style which included a different kind of buying — clothes to fit a career, a microwave for quick dinners and a reliable car. Eight-year-old Jan didn't really understand the hows, whats and wherefores of child support. She had no way of knowing the money was not just for toys and games but to help pay for such fixed expenses as rent, utilities, insurance, clothing, etc. All she knew was that her Daddy sent her money and she never got to see any, let alone spend it!

On a Saturday afternoon shopping trip, and after three "no's" followed by her Mother buying a new dress, Jan blurted out, "You spend the money Daddy sends me on you!" How her Mother interprets and responds to this comment will determine whether or not a game is born. If she realizes that her daughter's criticism reflects a lack of understanding, a potential game can be laid to rest with an explanation which fits her level of maturity.

If Jan's statement is taken at face value without evaluating how she came to her conclusion, it may be seen and responded to as a game initiation. A typical game-stimulating response to a naive accusation such as Jan's is to become defensive and angry. To do so will fuel Jan's resentments and prime her for another outburst when she again hears a no to what she believes is a legitimate request. A further way to promote a game is to permit a youngster's outburst to hook into the Parent tape, "A good Mother sacrifices and does without for her children."

At the other end of the spectrum is the adolescent who comprehends the meaning and intent of support, yet accuses his mother of spending the support money on herself. In this instance the primary motivators are to provoke parental conflict or to intimidate and dominate.

Ronna is a 13-year-old whose acting out has reached such magnitude that her parents are considering sending her to boarding school. In an attempt to avoid this dreaded consequence, she threw out a "You Spent My Child Support." Ronna's accusation was double-edged. On the one hand it was designed to divert attention from herself by creating parental conflict. Secondly, it was a threat. She knew the support money was also a help to her Mother, and if she were sent away to school a portion of her Mother's income would leave with her. In effect she was saying, "Watch it, you are partially dependent upon me."

Single parents must become aware that children of divorce develop new and different ways of viewing money. Since X amount is specifically earmarked for them, they develop a vested interest in how it is spent and believe they have the *right* to control how it is used.

Dads aren't exempt from their children's new perceptions and beliefs either. If Johnnie and Janie don't have the bike, clothes or stereo they know they *should* have and see Dad buying for himself, they are quick to question his love as they search for his guilt button.

As divorced parents, find out about your children's new beliefs about money. With this awareness you will be less likely to respond defensively to your children's challenge and be in a better position to avoid a money game. If a youngster continues throwing out Cons, don't become defensive and fight back or you will end up in a game of "You Spent My Child Support."

DADDY WILL BUY IT

Children are likely to become "Daddy Will Buy It" players if:

There is a significant difference between each
 parent's standard of living.
The parents are angry at each other and have little or
 no communication about the children.

Donny, who was reared in an upper middle class home, was nine when his parents divorced three years ago. Although he didn't like moving from his house and leaving his big bedroom and the pool, at first it wasn't so bad. He had fun at his Dad's condominium, complete with tennis court, game room and two pools.

Over the years the differences in the way each parent lived and viewed the world made a deep impression on him. Dad bought lots of new and exciting things while Mom complained about the old furniture, the price of gasoline and the rising cost of food. Relative to his Mother, he saw his Father as rich and powerful. He envied the way his Dad lived and fantasized about all the things he could have and do if his parents were still married. The more he observed and fantasized, the angrier he became over the divorce.

When his Mother refused him an impulsive "buy me," he frequently went to his Father who, more often than not, bought it for him. Invariably he showed the gift to his Mother as if to say, "See all the different things I could have if you and Dad were still married."

After one too many "no's," and with the knowledge that Dad would probably buy it for him, he defiantly shouted, "Dad will buy it for me!" With that remark his Mother came unglued. She called him an ungrateful manipulator and accused his Father of trying to buy his love. On the inside she felt exasperated, frustrated and angry. She knew she couldn't compete with his Father materialistically, and she saw Donny turning into a deceitful spoiled brat over whom she was losing control. Since Donny's parents were not on speaking terms, they were unable to communicate and break this destructive chain of events.

Beneath Donny's Con, "Buy it for me," was the ulterior message, "Look at what I lost because you divorced." His Mother hooked into the game by exploding at Donny when he waved Dad's presents under her nose. Both were vulnerable to this kind of manipulation because of their anger at each other and their refusal to communicate. This game transaction seems to be prompted by two factors: Donny's anger over what he lost because of the divorce and his wish to make his parents pay for his unhappiness. There are several solutions available.

Since his Mother is the one who is aware of Donny's manipulation of both her and his Father, she should attempt to break the communication barrier with her ex-husband. If she can enlist his cooperation, they can jointly confront Donny with his behaviors and set appropriate limits for him. This would cut through the deceit and manipulation. If she is unable to gain his cooperation, her next option is to confront Donny alone from her Adult. Her statement should be to the effect that she is aware of what he is doing, disapproves of his behavior, is aware she has no control over his Father's behavior and therefore will no longer be threatened, angered, or available for blackmail. The adoption of this attitude may take the steam out of Donny and set the climate for a more open expression of feelings and thoughts. If this occurs, Donny might tell his Mother the real reason for his actions, "I could have a whole family and more things if you and Dad were still married."

If you hear a "Daddy Will Buy It For Me," beware! You are being manipulated by a child who needs two strong and *cooperative* parents. If your child is in charge of you, who's left to take care of him?

DOUBLE YOUR PLEASURE

Bonnie and Larry agreed that the kids would come first. For the kids this agreement turned into a succession of outings to Six Flags, the movies, the theater, the ball park, the zoo, the aquarium, boating, fishing, bowling, tennis and golf, not to mention two vacations, two birthday parties and two Christmases. For Bonnie and Larry it turned into a nightmare.

Soon after the divorce, as Bonnie began reorientating her life to the realities of work, single parenthood, and her own social needs, the agreement came back to haunt her. It mattered little what she had done, what she was planning, or how she felt — there were always the inevitable "take me's." Her first "No" to a Friday evening demand that she take them roller skating came tumbling out of her mouth after an exhausting week at her first job since before they were born. Her three children responded with shock and indignation. Feeling guilty and remembering the agreement, Bonnie gave in.

Her all too frequent and inappropriate "Yes's" to her little prince and princesses laid the foundation for her to be seen as the wicked queen mother. Another month of "take me's" and "do for me's" left her angry and frustrated and she overreacted by giving them a huge "No," (grounding them for a week) to a small and legitimate request. Bonnie paid for that no in spades. Whenever she asked them to go or to do for themselves they behaved as if she had betrayed them. After all, they had been primed for "Yes's."

Since Larry was only with them on weekends and vacations, he was able to keep the pace up longer. Seeing Dad as the good guy, they complained, "Mom never does anything with us." They told him how boring it was living with her. Because he was with them less, was lonely himself, and remembered the agreement, he re-doubled his efforts.

While on a skiing trip, like Bonnie, he bought the course. No matter what he planned or what they did it was never enough. They acted like babies demanding and expecting. Buckling boots and ski binders, retrieving gloves and goggles, and zipping and unzipping quickly got old. He kept hoping they would take some responsibility for tasks they were capable of doing. It remained just that, a hope.

He met a woman at the ski lodge and planned dinner with her *alone.* As with Bonnie, the children acted betrayed and demanded to be included. Guilt reared its ugly head and Larry, the kids and his date spent the evening discussing where Daddy would take his prince and princesses the next morning.

Relieved that the trip was over, Larry looked forward to a quiet weekend at home. Talking to his daughter over the phone and making no mention of plans for the weekend she insolently asked, "What are we going to do Sunday?" Larry answered, "Stay home," and she countered with an icy "goodby!" He hung up feeling used and resentful. He asked himself, "How could my own kids treat me this way?"

The trap Bonnie and Larry set for themselves was due to their guilt. At the onset of their separation, neither was thinking clearly and both were feeling guilty. Although their intent was to care for and protect their children, their feelings got in the way of clear thinking and realistic parenting. Larry and Bonnie paid for their guilt through excessive entertaining and acceding to constant demands. The children quickly learned to press their parents' guilt buttons to get and get and get. When they got they pulled the Switch with, "It's not good enough, you owe us more."

Divorced parents can unwittingly fall into this trap simply by virtue of their singleness. They do their best to maintain their parental status quo. The net effect is two single parents attempting to do and provide as if they were still married. The kids begin to expect, their expectations grow and their wants and demands multiply. Fun times two turns into "Double Your Pleasure."

LET'S MOM AND DAD FIGHT

Twelve-year-old Sherry thought her Dad was "King of the Mountain." Although her parents seldom argued loudly or openly, when they did, she became very upset at her mother and protective of her father. Sherry distorted what she saw and heard. She saw her father as the good guy, her mother as the bad guy, and the arguments louder, more frequent and more ferocious than they actually were.

A year later Ray and Mary, Sherry's parents, divorced. Both described it as a painful, though amicable divorce. "We had become strangers and decided to separate."

Sherry's first "about-face" was her reaction to her Father. She acted as though he couldn't even pour a glass of water right. Not only wasn't he "King of the Mountain," he wasn't even part of her kingdom. Had Ray been an inattentive parent he might have understood her reaction. However, he was a good single parent. He saw the kids regularly, paid sufficient child support, and actively participated in their lives. To add insult to injury, Sherry began giving her Mother blow by blow reports about her Dad. At first Mary suspected her reports were distorted, but eventually she bought the Con. She began taking Sherry's side and took her anger out on Ray through hateful phone calls and being uncooperative.

An example of one of Sherry's game initiations occurred when Ray took the kids to the beach. Ray had one beer at the beach and sipped a second in the car on the way home. Sherry told her mother, "Mom, I'm worried about Dad's drinking. It was scary riding home with him. He was even drinking in the car." Mary was hooked!

Had she stopped and thought she could have guessed something was amiss since Ray was a casual drinker and she had never seen him drunk. Instead, she angrily accused him of drinking too much and driving while drunk. When he replied, "That's untrue! I had two beers the whole day," Mary shot back, "My own kids wouldn't lie to me." Mary's accusing and Ray's defending turned into a Mexican stand-off.

Ray began treating Sherry like a hot potato! He couldn't understand her sudden dislike for him and found relating to her impossible. This kind of reaction from an adolescent daughter may be due to one or more of the following factors.

Oedipal Complex

According to psychoanalytic theory, the Oedipal stage is a phenomenon which all children experience at approximately five to six years of age. At this point in a child's psycho-sexual development, he or she develops a strong, though unconscious, sexual attachment to the opposite sex parent. With these feelings of rivalry go hateful and even murderous thoughts toward the same sex parent. If this were a conscious process, a male child might say, "I want Mom for myself and wish Dad would go away or die."

The resolution of the Oedipal stage occurs when the child accepts the fact that the opposite sex parent is already taken and identifies with the same sex parent, i.e.,"I'll be a man and find a girl for myself just like Dad did." During adolescence a youngster re-experiences, though less intensely, the Oedipal phase.

It is possible that Sherry's father's availability, as a result of the divorce, was so threatening that she reacted against these forbidden and unconscious wishes by behaving negatively toward him.

Balancing Loyalties

Many children take one parent's side over the other. Their reasons may be valid, the result of parental brainwashing, or due to a child's own needs, wants and perceptions.

Sherry had always sided with her father. To continue doing so while in her mother's custody could have been too threatening. Her negative stance toward her father may have been her way of balancing the scales of loyalty and endearing herself to her mother.

The Pedestal Syndrome

Sherry had a distorted view of her father. She endowed him with more power, wisdom and authority than any father could possibly live up to. That *he permitted* this catastrophe, the divorce, left her hurt, angry and disillusioned. Her response to his humanness and fall from the pedestal, on which she had placed him, may have been to turn against him.

As with most games the solution lies in open, honest communication. Had her parents shared their perceptions and thoughts about Sherry they would have been united, alert and sensitive to Sherry's behavior and could have reduced the chances of accepting a game invitation. If she continued to pit them against each other, they would have been in a position to know the truth, protect themselves or, if necessary, seek professional help.

WANNA PLAY HOUSE?

Roberta was furious at her fifteen-year-old daughter Robin. "It's disgusting the way she rushes over to clean her Father's apartment when she won't even pick her own clothes up off the floor. If I say anything, ANYTHING, she accuses me of attacking her Dad. They act like they're playing house."

Robin's Dad, Jack, went straight from Momma to wife and spent the last twenty years in a traditional male dominant-female dependent marriage. Jack turned out to be a first class clod when it came to running a household. He never cleaned, did the wash or cooked. Seldom did he eat or sleep in his apartment unless he was with Robin or some other female.

Robin was, and had always been, the light of his life. When Roberta spoke to him about Robin's role in his life, he became angry at her for questioning what he considered a healthy father-daughter relationship.

Robin's stance toward her Father is not atypical. A motherly-wifely relationship between divorced fathers and their daughters is prompted by one or both of the following factors.

Cultural Scripting

Little girls are taught to be dependent nurturers. Little boys are taught to be occupationally potent and domestically dependent. This set of circumstances makes it almost natural for fathers to permit their daughters to take over where their mothers and ex-wives left off. It is also an easy matter for daughters to slide into this role.

The Oedipal Complex

Teenage daughters can act out their unconscious desire for their father by becoming a surrogate wife. Divorced fathers with teenage daughters must be aware of the fine line they are walking. On the one hand, they should not discount or totally refuse their daughters' attempts to help them. Girls practice being a woman with their fathers. On the other hand, they should not let a daughter play act at being what she is not — a wife.

For his own well being, it is essential that Jack learn to provide for his own domestic needs. Since he also plays a significant role in Robin's scripting, it is equally important that he provide her with an adequate male model, domestically as well as occupationally. By viewing men as able to care for their own wants and needs it is less likely that Robin will adopt and perpetuate the cultural myth that a woman's role is to take care of others at her own personal, social and occupational expense.

The following was our reply to one teacher's letter as she wrote of her frustrations in dealing with students whose parents are divorced.

> You and the school are important sources of consistency, stability and security to a child whose life has suddenly been turned topsy turvy. We advise divorcing parents to keep their children's lives as unchanged as possible. The same applies to the school.

> During the initial period of crisis, when their parents physically separate, most children find it difficult to handle the academic and social responsibilities of school. Some withdraw, become aggressive, or regress to an earlier stage of development. Others continue on, as if nothing had happened, and silently shoulder their hurt. Youngsters who exhibited learning or behavioral problems before the separation may do even worse. Most return to their normal level of functioning within a few months.

> Don't let your students play Wooden Leg, i.e., "What do you expect from a kid whose parents are divorcing?" Counter their excuses with a firm, yet understanding, statement to the effect you expect their assignments completed. This is not being punitive or harsh. Rather, you are providing an important source of consistency and reality.

> If a child continues offering excuses, talk to his parents. During the conference:
> - Report the child's behavior objectively without making value judgments or diagnoses.
> - Don't ask questions which are irrelevant to a student's progress at school.
> - Don't place yourself, even if invited, in the position of therapist to student or parent.
> - Tell them that your school psychologist and counselor are excellent referral sources.

As a single parent are you working against yourself? Check yourself out.

1. Are you taking care of you? If you don't function well, little else will!

2. Has the *leveling process* occurred and, if so, how have you dealt with it? Leveling refers to the fact that without the presence and support of another adult in the household, the authority gap between children and the single parent narrows so that children attempt to bargain and negotiate over every little issue and task.

3. Have you learned to balance the social and occupational demands for your time and energy with those placed on you by your children?

4. Do you stroke your children intensely and frequently enough so as to keep their batteries charged and the need for negative strokes through game transactions down?

5. Do you sometimes do for the children for the express purpose of "out-doing" their other parent?

6. Do you feel guilty over the divorce and try to make it up to the children?

7. Do you think, want, or attempt to change your children's relationship with your ex-spouse?

8. Do you sometimes feel angry or resentful over the responsibility of single parenthood? If so, how do you show it?

9. Have you impeded your ex-spouse's effectiveness in parenting by being uncooperative?

If you are in this situation, be aware of its potential to develop into a game, particularly if you are playing helpless and permitting your daughter to play wife and mother.

NO HOMEWORK

Children are quick to pick up on society's response and attitudes toward divorce. Elise, an eleven-year-old, told us how easy it is to get out of doing things, especially homework, if your parents are divorced. "All I have to do is tell my teacher I had to go to Dad's last night or that I couldn't get my homework done because I had to babysit my brother."

Because of her poor grades and insolent attitude, Elise's Mother brought her for counseling. Her explanation of the problem began with, *"Poor Elise,* she's been through a lot the past couple of months." Her teacher summed up the situation with, "This *poor child's* parents are divorced and she's been tossed around like a ball. It's no wonder she's not doing well in school!"

The opportunity for Elise to manipulate was, in large measure, made possible because of society's expectations of the difficulties a child of divorce *must* experience. This has led to and reinforced a cultural game of Wooden Leg. As described by Eric Berne, Wooden Leg is a game in which the initiator disclaims responsibility for an action or inaction because of some defect, problem or disability. Because of the apparent plausibility of the excuse, others join in and support the Wooden Leg player.

A child of divorce initiates the game with the Con, "I can't." The ulterior message is, "What do you expect — my parents are divorced." The Con is accepted because it fits with society's Gimmick, *"Poor you,* you come from a broken home." This attitude strokes the child for being a helpless victim and promotes further irresponsible behaviors. The Switch occurs when, after getting his way, another demand or excuse is made.

Elise opened her game of "No Homework" with, "I couldn't do my homework because . . ." Her ulterior motive was, "What do you expect of a child from a broken home?" Her teacher's Gimmick was her belief and expectation that children of divorce are too fragile and traumatized to behave normally. She responded to Elise by giving her too many extra chances. When she failed, Elise pulled the Switch with, "If you had helped me more, I wouldn't have failed." Her Payoff was to feel indignant and misunderstood, "I told you, I was from a broken home." Her teacher's Payoff was guilt (I should have helped her more), failure (I failed as a teacher), and confusion (what happened?). The more she "tried" to help, the more helpless and less responsible Elise became.

Divorce is a crisis in the lives of all children. For awhile they may have difficulty concentrating, their motivation toward school may dwindle, some become behavior problems and others refuse to go to school for fear the custody parent will also leave them. Still others are concerned about what their teachers will say and whether or not their friends will be allowed to play with them since they are now a "divorced kid."

These concerns and reactions are, for the most part, short-lived. If a child continues to behave differently from his old self or sustains a game of academic Wooden Leg, his teacher should speak to his parents and/or make a referral to the school counselor. If necessary, an evaluation by a psychologist should be sought.

The following interviews reprinted from our newspaper column will give you an idea of two children's views of divorce.

Mel, I had the most charming date! Just listen to these statistics: Brown twinkly eyes, curly hair, smooth olive complexion and intelligent. Problem was he was only seven years old. Believe it or not we talked for a whole hour on divorce. He is a well-adjusted child whose parents have been divorced two years.

He opened our conversation by asking, "Why do people want to get divorced?" He went on to explain, "Divorce is no good because people don't live together anymore, and you don't have anyone waiting at home to hug and kiss." He still hasn't told his school chums his parents are divorced. He doesn't like the word divorce because it means, "Two people separating from the same house."

He thought it wasn't fair that, "Mom gets two big closets, and Dad has only one in his apartment." He didn't like his Mom working because, "She doesn't have time to clean the house like she used to." He felt, "It's not fair Dads have to work until seven or six, and they never get to clean up their apartment." He didn't like having to help his Dad clean up.

I asked if he saw anything good about divorce and he replied, "There is more room in the garage for my bike (just one car now), and Mom has to cook less."

He thought Dads wouldn't miss their kids if they called four times a week and visited twice. He wondered if

Dads missed Moms, but decided if they had kids to pick up they wouldn't. He didn't feel he had any problems and thanked me for the peanut butter break.

Brenda, a 14-year-old, lives and attends school in an affluent neighborhood. She makes average grades, has never been in serious trouble, and her parents have been divorced four years. She lives with her mother and visits her father weekly. We began the interview by citing research that showed that the problems of children whose parents are divorced are not any more frequent or serious than those of children whose parents are married.

Brenda responded, "I think kids with divorced parents tend to be losers more than other kids." We asked why and she answered, "If mothers with custody need to work, they come home so tired that while they might care about their kids it seems like they don't. Lots of times working mothers are blind to what their kids are doing and their kids aren't about to tell them!"

She continued to focus on the custody parent being overtired from work. "I know one kid whose mother was asleep so he and his friends slipped out of the house and stole her car. They drove around without a driver's license, smoked pot and didn't come back until 5 A.M. and his mother never knew it. One girl brought some kids home to spend the night after her mother was asleep. They locked the bedroom door and when she left for work the next morning she never even checked her daughter's room."

She seemed fascinated with staying out at night and told us how it was done. "I would say I am spending the night with Barbara and Barbara would tell her mother she was spending the night with me. If we got tired we would go to the laundromat and sleep for a couple of hours."

Her next statement reflected an important idea. "One parent isn't as strict as two, so it's harder for me to say no to something my friends want to do. When I tell them no, they say, 'Oh, your mother's working so she won't know.' There is a lot of pressure on me to keep all these things a secret."

She discussed the differences she saw between kids whose parents are and are not divorced. "Kids whose parents aren't divorced are stuck up and won't mix with us. They get away with a lot, too. Because their parents think they're good-ies and the kids take advantage of them. No one ever sus-pects them of anything! Some are nice at school so you wouldn't know they go out and get drunk Friday nights. At the city recreation center they bring a drink called 'mad dog.' It's made with brandy and other stuff they steal from their parents."

She saw kids from single-parent homes as poorly dressed. We asked her about the in sloppy look and she quickly retorted, "Yea, but the other kids have an expensive sloppy look." She was almost sure none of the cheerleaders' parents were divorced and believed kids from single-parent homes weren't very involved in school activities. Besides, she said, "It's real easy for a kid with just one parent to play hookey."

She went on, "There's a Seven Eleven close to our school and a lot of my friends shoplift there, particularly cigarettes." We inquired about their ethics and she said, "Well, some of their parents have been divorced since they were two and they never had time to teach them any." She believes that kids whose parents are divorced do riskier things, like smoke pot.

Suddenly a positive aspect emerged as she noted that a kid whose parents are divorced learns to take responsibility like washing clothes, learning to cook, and being aware of what things cost. She said, "Later on I will have it over the stuck up kids because I will know how to do more things in the adult world."

We were left with a big view of a little part of her world.

7

RENT-A-KID

Chapter 6 dealt with games initiated by children. This chapter will focus on parent-initiated games.

THE WISHBONE EFFECT

Being pulled, torn and stretched between parents is one of the most difficult experiences a child of divorce will ever encounter. While at one time or other most children lean more toward one parent or the other, to children whose parents are divorced the meaning and intensity of these feelings are different and heightened.

Divided loyalties, or the wishbone effect, stem from numerous sources.

1. Whether they admit it or not or are aware of it or not, most parents secretly want their children to *like* them best. Love is not the issue. The internal dialogue goes something like, "It's all right for little George to love his Dad as much as me, but I want him to like me best." It is as if love is biologically determined while liking is a voluntary act which makes a statement about a person's worth as a parent.

2. After divorce conflict between parents tends to polarize children's feelings and create divided loyalties. Youngsters see what they want to see, hear what they

want to hear, make their interpretations and take sides. Right or wrong isn't the issue. The point is they take sides. The potential for divided loyalties and after divorce games between parents and children is enhanced when parents remain at war with one another.

3. Putting down or discounting the other parent in front of children is a prime way of creating distance between parents and children. Whether said over legitimate issues or out of maliciousness, in either event, it is often done to cleanse oneself in the eyes of the children, for any responsibility for the divorce.

4. The ego state out of which a parent refers to or speaks about the other parent conveys a host of meanings. Messages about guilt, blame, and fault are communicated as clearly by facial expression, gestures, posture and tone of voice as they are by word. The sentence, "You know how your Dad is so you will have to decide what to do," has many different meanings depending upon the ego state from which it is said. Spoken from the Adult it is a statement of fact and a request for a decision. Stated from the Critical Parent it is a negative value judgment. If said from the rebellious part of the Adapted Child it could be a signal to fight.

5. All children want to see and believe that their parents are good, and as a result they tend to over idealize and view them as larger than life. The often heard, "My Daddy is stronger than yours," is a classic example. Therefore, it is not surprising that a child will align himself with the maligned parent in an attempt to protect his image of that parent.

    We have dealt with scores of youngsters who have run to the defense of a parent even when they secretly knew Mom or Dad was wrong. The psychology here is relatively straightforward. Most children identify very closely with their parents; therefore, to attack a parent is like attacking them. Without an understanding of this process, a child's reactions can

prove confusing, frustrating and exasperating to a
parent whose children become angry at them for
making an accurate, though negative, comment
about their other parent.

The following letter from an "After Divorce"
reader illustrates this point.

"In the three years since my divorce my ex-
husband has been extremely unreliable about visiting
the children and sending child support. On two occasions I have had to take legal steps to collect the back
child support. Sometimes my anger gets the best of
me and I say something bad about their father to the
kids. Even though they know what I'm saying is true,
they jump to his defense and turn on me like I'm the
bad guy."

6. Conflict over visitation can stimulate feelings of divided loyalties. This kind of conflict is more apt to occur if the terms of the visitation agreement have not
   been *legally* spelled out and *clearly* defined. It is traumatic for a child to see his parents fighting over who
   "gets him" Christmas, Thanksgiving, etc. Either way
   he loses.

7. Significant differences in standards of living can be
   another sore spot. Some children become angry and
   antagonistic if they and their custody parent have to
   live beneath the economic level of the non-custody
   parent. Children often resent the life style of the
   wealthier parent and, at the same time, wish to live
   that life style. The resultant effect is confusion and
   ambivalence.

8. The presence of a stepparent can also lead to intense
   feelings of divided loyalties.

WISHBONE

Jonathan and Terri's parents have been divorced four
years. Although the divorce was amicable, both Wayne and
Joyce experienced intense pain and anguish. Through it all
they kept the children's well-being in the forefront and sup-

ported them and each other at every opportunity. Wayne stayed in close contact with Joyce and the children and was emotionally and financially reliable.

As Wayne and Joyce emotionally unhooked, they developed different ways of viewing their worlds. Nonetheless they managed to remain in essential agreement as to what was best for the children. As the years passed the children adopted their mother's way of thinking, behaving and doing. Ever so slowly they began viewing their father as not only different, but wrong.

Wayne discovered there was little he could do that was not viewed with suspicion, or distrust, or as just plain wrong. Believing their father was unshakable in his inaccurate beliefs, the kids didn't talk to him about his actions or "strange" ways. Instead, they went to their mother with their complaints. In the beginning, Joyce listened briefly and then referred them back to their father. As personal and parental philosophies grew more and more divergent, and acting out of the belief that Wayne's problems with the children were none of her business, seldom did she encourage them to speak to their father or alert Wayne as to what was happening. What she did do was listen longer and longer.

For nearly a year Wayne knew something was amiss but couldn't put his finger on it. When he shared his impressions and frustrations with Joyce, she responded, "I won't get in the middle between you and the kids. You'll have to work it out between yourselves." Joyce's behavior did not fit her words. By listening to their complaints she was not letting them work it out between themselves; instead, she was reinforcing the children's beliefs about Wayne. Her ulterior motive was, "Like me better." Wayne's Gimmick was feelings of parental inadequacy and the fear that if he confronted the children they might reject him. When he spoke to Joyce she pulled the Switch with, "That's your problem." Joyce's Payoff was to feel one up and the better parent. Wayne's was to feel alone, sad and martyred.

The key to avoiding a game of Wishbone is to give up the desire to be the favored parent. It is important for children of divorce to learn that different people have different ways.

RENT-A-KID

"I was furious as usual when my ex was late picking up our daughter. I called him and don't remember exactly what I said, but when I hung up my daughter said, 'You sound just like a Rent-A-Kid service." Angry at herself for losing her cool and at her husband for behaving like a rat, Norma continued, "There I sat with my daughter telling me I treated her like a piece of property."

Since her parents' divorce, Crissie felt like an object, something to be used at someone else's convenience. She said, "My Mom wants to get rid of me so she can go out and have fun. She tries to pawn me off on my Dad. My Dad wants to see me when it suits him. It's like I'm worth 24-hours to the gallon. Maybe I should wear a sign, 'Kid for Rent Weekends — Cheap.' "

When Norma and Hal divorced they reassured Crissie that they were still her parents and would not abandon her. This is hardly the scene they portrayed as they argued over who would keep her on weekends. The harder they fought for their "free" weekend, the angrier, more left out and unloved she felt.

Hal had not unhooked from Norma and was using many of the same tactics to control her that he had used during their marriage. When they were married the watchword was inconsistency. He was early, late or didn't show. Instead of going alone or making separate plans, like a good wife she waited for Hal. After the divorce Hal was inconsistent in seeing Crissie. As in her marriage Norma played the good little ex-wife and made her plans around Hal.

As Norma emotionally separated from Hal and began creating an independent life, she wanted some free time for herself. She loved her daughter, but working full-time and being a parent 100% of the time left her feeling stale and hollow. For at least brief periods, she wanted a break from full-time motherhood.

Her false belief that Hal held the key to her personal and social freedom kept her in a box and a victim of his capriciousness. Where in the divorce papers does it say that a mother must only go out when her ex-husband is supposed to be with the children? Where does it say that mothers *must* depend on fathers in order to have free time?

Because Norma bought into these beliefs, she set herself up for unneeded tension and stress which bled over into her relationship with Crissie. Hal was behaving just as unreliably as he had before the divorce, and Norma could have predicted this. That she hung onto her false belief and did not probability estimate Hal's after divorce behavior, tells us this is a set-up for a game.

Had Norma predicted Hal's behavior and taken control by not centering her schedule around him, her frustration and resentment would not have built to the point that she felt trapped by her own daughter.

POOPER-SCOOPER

Like most wives of up and coming executives, Linda had her own car, a closet full of clothes, and a four bedroom house complete with swimming pool and mortgage to match. When she divorced she received her share of what the bank didn't own, which included her clothes, most of the furniture and her sons age 11 and 13. Her Cadillac, like Cinderella's carriage, turned into a pumpkin sized sub-compact. Her spacious home was replaced with a "quaint," but smallish duplex with a postage stamp for a back yard.

With the duplex brimming over with furnishings from a rambling ranch style house, for awhile everyone was bumping into or squeezing by someone or something. Nonetheless, they were comfortable and were not what you could remotely call deprived. Still, the change in life style was difficult for Linda to adjust to. While her boys seemed to be doing fine, Linda held onto the nagging feeling that by divorcing their father she had deprived them of many of the niceties of life they would have had coming.

Feeling badly about what she "had done" to the kids and putting guilt in front of common sense, she suggested they get a pet. Agreeing on a *small* dog, off to the pound they went in search of a miniature Fido. The boys picked out an adorable mongrel with paws the size of saucers. Seeing the handwriting on the wall, Linda reminded them of their agreement (a small dog) and explained that a puppy with paws that size would probably grow up and up and up! The boys protested exclaiming they had fallen in love with Poopsie and that Poopsie had fallen in love with them. Guilt prevailed and home they went with Poopsie.

Poopsie was a healthy, thriving puppy. In fact, the way she grew Linda wondered if she wasn't part horse. Poopsie had a ravenous appetite. She ate the center cushion of the sofa, a dining room table leg and Linda's new shoes. She barked during the day and throughout most of the night. Poopsie poo-pooed everywhere. Poopsie soon outgrew the yard and could easily burrow under or scale over the fence. Poopsie delighted in playing hide and ye shall seek.

The boys were visiting their father the day Poopsie knocked over Linda's prize plant and rolled in the dirt scattering it all over the living room. Finding the mess, Linda flew into a wall-eyed rage and loaded 80 lbs. of dog into her pumpkin sized car and off to the pound they went! Returning home to find their beloved Poopsie gone, the boys screamed, "You lied to us. You told us we could have a dog. Dad would have let us keep Poopsie."

This entire series of gamey transactions was initiated out of Linda's irrational feelings of guilt. Her Con was suggesting the dog. Her ulterior motive was to please the boys in order to relieve her guilt over the divorce. Linda set the stage for the Switch, returning the dog, by agreeing to a pet which obviously did not fit with their living arrangements. Her Payoff was to feel increased guilt, martyred, and less adequate as a mother and single parent. The boys' Payoff was hurt, anger and distrust of their Mother.

In Linda's case the overt game transaction centered about a pet. Pooper-Scooper may have more meaning for you if you view it as a representative example of a game transaction prompted by irrational guilt. In your case it could center around an expensive vacation, a private school, or a very much wanted but unneeded car for a teenager.

SPECTATOR SPORT

Sean and Marci were banged up and scarred after two marriages and two divorces, both to each other. Control, money and sex games had been their history. Their after divorce relationship was no different.

Sean kept his money games alive by diverting and hiding assets in order to minimize "his losses" in the property and alimony settlements. He kept his control games alive by using his business activities (travel) as a ruse to avoid committing to a regular visitation schedule. This tack permitted him to visit Ali, their ten-year-old daughter, when it suited him, as well as to make it difficult for Marci to plan her schedule. Seldom, if ever, did he see Ali on weekends. To do so would have given Marci the freedom to plan her weekends without babysitters and the luxury of being alone with a man in her home.

Believing she got "Screwed in the Settlement," Marci did her damnedest to hook into and aggravate Sean's money games. Even though she was short on cash, she foiled opportunity after opportunity to sell some property which, after its sale, was to be divided between them. Since the settlement agreement stipulated that Sean was to be responsible for the bank notes, this seemed a perfect way to get back at him.

Though they were extremely angry at each other, Marci still cared for Sean and harbored the wish that they could somehow reconcile. Aware of Marci's feelings, Sean kept her off balance with innuendos that a reconciliation might be possible.

The forgotten party was Ali. She couldn't understand why her Dad treated her Mom so badly, why he lived so much better than they, and why he didn't see her regularly. Mad at her dad for being "mean" to her mom and expecting her to see him whenever he called, Ali began lying to avoid visiting him — "I can't have dinner with you, I'm going to a slumber party tonight." Needing some relief from single parenthood, believing Ali needed her father and with some pressure from Sean, Marci pushed Ali to see her dad.

Amidst all the other ongoing games, the stage was set for a game of "Spectator Sport." When Ali visited with her Dad, be it at a restaurant or his apartment, she was more of a spectator than a participant. Seldom did they do anything or go anywhere without her dad bringing along a date. Ali felt repulsed when she saw her father and his date hold hands, hug or sneak kisses. She wondered why he was so affectionate with these strange women and was so cold to her mom.

Her anger and confusion reached the point that she refused to see her father. Marci attempted to persuade her to see him until Ali dropped the bombshell. She told her mom how her father acted with other women. Still hooked into Sean, Marci was shaken. She permitted Ali to stop seeing her dad and angrily called Sean telling him how his behavior with other women was hurting his relationship with Ali. Sean responded, "It's none of your damn business and I'll see my daughter whenever I want."

Sean's Con was the claim that he wanted to visit Ali. His ulterior motive was, "Watch and tell your mother how good I'm doing without her." Marci's Gimmick was her emotional ties to Sean and hopes of reconciliation. When she responded angrily, Sean pulled the Switch with, "We're divorced, and it's none of your damn business what I do. If you don't like it you can go to hell!" However, Sean had made it Marci's business by behaving the way he did in front of Ali.

Sean's Payoff was vengeful anger. Marci's was to question her lovability and femininity and to feel angry and inadequate. Ali felt confused, angry and betrayed.

Marci participated in the game because of her refusal to unhook from Sean. Two bad marriages and two bouts of after divorce warfare with the same man should have been enough. Had she unhooked, she would have taken affirmative legal action to arrange an appropriate visitation schedule. Instead she took up the role of martyr. Had she unhooked, she would have sold the property and severed her business ties with Sean. Had she unhooked, it is doubtful he would have attempted to get back at her through other women. If he had, with no response from her, it is unlikely he would have continued since it netted him little in the way of vengeful satisfaction.

Sean also needed to unhook. Although he no longer wanted a loving or romantic relationship with Marci, his anger kept him just as hooked into her as if he loved and wanted her. The final product was, and still is, an ongoing series of painful game transactions with Ali in the middle.

JIMMY AND THE BEANSTALK

Jimmy, a junior high school student, seemed headed in the wrong direction. He spent more than his share of time in the principal's office, his grades were poor, and he refused to become involved in school activities. He explained to his mom that the kids at school divided themselves into three groups. While the vagueness of his definitions made it hard for his mother to distinguish one group from the other, to the kids it was crystal clear. A *Social* is supposedly a rich snob, who is active in school affairs and secretly drinks beer and smokes pot. A *Freak* can be rich or poor, smoke pot openly and defiantly, and dress like a slob. A *Jock* can be rich or poor, is involved in athletics and seldom uses pot. Disavowing labels, Jimmy labeled himself an *In between.*

In between was an accurate description of Jimmy. If you knew him you might have wondered if he was coming or going. One moment he was full of "yes ma'am's" and the next was throwing a tantrum or threatening to run away if he didn't get his way. His mood swings and erratic behavior were exasperating and sometimes frightening to his mother.

To understand Jimmy you need to understand his parents. His father was an eccentric, "me-centered" person whose primary aim in life was to make a million dollars. Even before the divorce the mood and attitude of the family seemed to rise and fall with his dad's financial windfalls and setbacks. At the time Jimmy was too young to comprehend the reasons for his father's behavior, and his confusion heightened as he found it harder and harder to predict his father's moods and what would please or anger him. In grade

school Jimmy developed the notion that there was some sort
of magic that determined his destiny.

His mother's reaction to his father reinforced his belief in
magic because, like him, she never seemed to know what was
in store for her. One evening he would be warm and loving
and the next wouldn't even bother to call and tell her he
wouldn't be home. There was only one for sure — Dad made
and controlled the money. If his father wanted a new
Mercedes it was in the driveway the next morning. If he or his
mom wanted something they had to "act right." The question
became, "What is right?"

After the divorce his dad spread money around like butter and 14-year-old Jimmy drooled over what might be coming his way. He and his mother were living well, but there were
no trips to the West Indies, sports cars or a vacation home in
Cape Cod. The difference in standards of living got to Jimmy
as he began resenting his life style with his Mother. Dad became the goose that laid the golden eggs.

For a year or so after the divorce, Jimmy and his father
saw quite a bit of each other. Liz, his mother, was happy about
this as she had anticipated Hank would stay wrapped up in his
tinsel world and forget about Jimmy. However, the mixed
messages he sent Jimmy began paying negative dividends
and magical thoughts compounded the interest.

In the eighth grade Jimmy's grades began their downhill
slide, he became argumentative and acted like the world
owed him. Liz caught him smoking pot and figured out that
the plants growing in his window sill, supposedly a botany
project, were marijuana. She responded angrily, set firmer
limits and discussed the situation with his dad. Hank agreed
that Jimmy would have to straighten up, and read him the
riot act.

Jimmy was confused. Somehow he had again stumbled
over that invisible magic line. He told his mom, "The first
time I smoked pot was at a party Dad gave. He saw me and
didn't say anything. He even keeps a 'lid' in a brandy snifter in
the bookcase." He went on to tell her that the fancy "roach
clip" his principal took away from him was a gift from one of

his dad's girl friends. Not wanting to anger the goose that laid the golden eggs, he tucked away his confusion and, for a while, cooled it with pot.

Jimmy's next escapade was to sneak out of the house late at night and take his friends cruising in his mother's car. When Liz discovered that her car had burned half a tank of gas while supposedly sitting in the garage, she put two and two together. Again she confronted Jimmy and spoke to his father. This turned out to be a repeat performance of the pot scene. Hank reprimanded Jimmy by withholding the golden eggs. Angry and confused Jimmy confided to his mother that his dad had been letting him drive his car for months. Unwittingly, Jimmy had again crossed that magic line. What he failed to understand was that the magic was really his Father's irrationality: It is all right to break the law one way, but not another way. It's all right to smoke pot "here," but it's wrong to smoke it "there." It's all right to drive without a license, but it's wrong to take your mother's car.

Jimmy was one mixed up 14-year-old. Because what he did took on different meanings and had different consequences at different times, his perception of his father was extremely confused. On the one hand he saw him as a wicked giant in need of slaying, and on the other as the possessor of those very much wanted golden eggs.

There was yet another aspect of his father's behavior which he found confusing. The golden eggs he dispensed were frequently tarnished. Upon receiving an egg he was particularly hungry for, his father would tell him about an even bigger and shinier one. This left Jimmy feeling let down, unsatisfied and hungry for the next one. His appetite became insatiable.

Hank's Con was, "I have an egg for you." The ulterior motive was, "Guess which hand it is in." The double messages he sent permitted a double Switch which left Jimmy in a corner. If Jimmy guessed right he was awarded a tarnished egg. If he guessed wrong the eggs were temporarily withheld. From Jimmy's point of view, the eggs appeared without rhyme or reason — that invisible magic line.

The aim of the game was power. Hank's Payoff was control and righteous indignation when his son did not act properly. Jimmy's Payoff was to feel stupid, confused and angry.

Hank also pulled the Switch on Liz. With one hand he supported her opinions, judgments and discipline of Jimmy and with the other swatted them away with behaviors which encouraged Jimmy's acting out.

Since Liz could not count on Hank, she should have set her own ground rules with Jimmy. She could have asked, "Who would pay the penalty if the police caught you driving without a license, even if you had your father's permission?" Having been invited into his Adult through the use of a question, Jimmy would have been in a position to explore his father's behaviors (the Con and Switch) and his behaviors (the Response and Gimmick). By processing behaviors and consequences through his Adult, Jimmy's confusion would have evaporated, his options would have been visible, and the choice to stay or leave the game *his*.

WE HAVE TO AT HOME, WHY DO WE HERE?

After his divorce, it didn't take Curtis long to figure out that a two bedroom apartment wouldn't work. Although his 14-year-old son and 12-year-old daughter were only with him weekends and vacations, the cramped apartment looked, felt and smelled more like a sardine can than a home.

Although the divorce cost him dearly, and even with the inflated price of houses and soaring interest rates, Curtis set out to recreate his dream of family, house and yard. He bought a house to fit this dream more than it did reality. Twenty-five hundred square feet of house may be perfect for a family of four, but is expensive, large and lonely for a family of one, except on weekends.

Filled with hope and excitement, Curtis helped the kids decorate their rooms, complete with posters, T.V., and stereo. The weekends were jammed with shopping, fixing up, and putting things in order.

Come spring, Curtis was raring to go. Early one Saturday morning he roared, "Rise and shine, let's get some breakfast so we can get to the yard!" With a chorus of sleepy moans and groans in the background, Curtis fried some sausage and eggs and herded the kids outside before they could get in another sleepy blink. The cool morning breeze, the smell of grass clippings, and the sound of the mower rekindled in Curtis the familiar ties to community and family. The scene held a different meaning for the kids — being shackled to the mower and slaves to the constant invasion of weeds and insects.

By early July the kids began their grumblings in earnest. Family chores, that bit of stickum which Curtis hoped would unite individuals into a cohesive family unit, turned into Krazy Glue. The kids' response to Curtis's attempts to create a family atmosphere was, "Oh, Dad we have to do that at home. Do we have to do it here, too?" Curtis was angered at their attitudes as well as their reference to their mother's house as *home*. He felt that they didn't understand or appreciate what he was doing for them.

Later that summer his ex-wife remarried Mr. Fix-It. He could build, plumb and garden like you wouldn't believe. Mr. Fix-It delighted in his five-year plan to revitalize the house. Hedges, trees and grass became his Saturday afternoon delight.

Used to, "Dad, we have to do it at home," Curtis was startled when he heard, "Dad we don't have to do that at home, why do we here?" That was the straw that broke the camel's back. He blew up and told them he didn't want to see them again until they straightened out.

Feeling sad, alone and unappreciated in that "family house" for one, he answered the phone one evening only to hear his ex-wife say, "Who do you think you are using the kids to do your yard work? They're not sharecroppers!" Searching for something to say and a way to make sense out of it all, he heard her click off abruptly.

Curtis's attempts to create a home for himself and his children failed on several accounts. His first error was to assume that his children held the same expectations as he, and that he could recreate in 48 hours the same environment, atmosphere and attitudes that existed when he was married to their mother. The ulterior message behind Curtis's "Rise and shine . . ." was, "Let's be a family like before so I can feel good again." When the children responded with moans and groans and complained to their mother, he pulled the Switch by threatening to abandon them.

Single non-custody parents can avoid this kind of game transaction by being aware of present realities, their own expectations and how they fit with those of their children. Awareness of personal and parental priorities is necessary. The idea is to meld, within the time available, what you want and what the kids want into a workable part-time living arrangement.

Curtis set himself up for unnecessary hurt and game transactions with his attempts to make things like they were before the divorce. His children's refusal to accept his expectations resulted in his Payoff, deep-seated feelings of sadness, loneliness, and rejection. To buy a home because one wants to is fine. To buy one in the hopes that it will make things like they were before is to ignore reality.

The call Curtis received from his ex-wife was patently inappropriate. Whether she was misinformed or insensitive was not the issue. The issue was Curtis's expectations, which rendered him vulnerable to this kind of attack. Had he evaluated the realities of part-time parenting, compared his wants and feelings with those of his children, and created a new type of family structure, the game might never have come into being.

MOMMA BOSS

Maggie ran her family like her business, with an iron hand. As the matriarch of the family and business, in ten short years she tripled their profits and acquired an extensive real estate portfolio which included an apartment complex, an office building and several hundred acres of prime raw land. By the age of 60 she had made her mark and had no intentions of slowing down.

Much of Maggie's drive and energy was derived from sublimated hate and anger. She was 50 when her husband left her for that "cheap hussy" half his age. On the outside she called him a sniveling idiot and spoke of her good fortune to be rid of him. On the inside she seethed and wouldn't forgive him for what he had done to her. She became intent on showing the world how much better and more capable she was than he.

At the time of her divorce her two sons were in their 20's. They had college degrees and had inherited her head for business, so *she decided* she would make them her partners. The boys had a little of the devil in them, just like their dad. Though they had exquisite wives, they were known to dance a jig or two with a barmaid after downing a few too many at the local lounge.

Maggie was aware of her sons' "extracurricular activities" and often told them, "Stop it, or you're going to end up just like your Father." The ever so slight tug at the corners of her mouth and her tone of voice were dead giveaways to the secret message, "Be like your dad." The boys obliged with a mistress or two.

When she saw her sons carrying things a bit too far, she would alert her daughters-in-law that their husbands were less than angels. She often told them, "Leave them while you are still young." The wives responded by fighting with their husbands, which gave Momma the opening she needed to call her sons on the carpet and warn them, "They're going to leave you if you don't shape up."

Despite the constant threats of separation and divorce, everyone knew they were empty and hollow. Momma Boss let the boys stray only so far before she pulled in the string. When she did, the guilt gifts that followed were just too good for their wives to pass by.

Maggie played both ends against the middle by prompting her sons to be like Dad, and then tattling to their wives. Her behavior initiated a game of "Let's You and Him Fight." However, Maggie was into something more than a simple game of "Let's You and Him Fight." The real motivator was Maggie's anger at her ex-husband, her fear of rejection, and her desire for control. She recreated with her sons and daughters-in-law her own history, and then stepped in as the rescuer to stop the proceedings before they got out of hand.

Her warning, "You'll end up like your father," was her

Con, which veiled the ulterior message, "Be like Dad." When her sons behaved like she had unconsciously instructed them, she pulled the Switch by slapping their hands and tattling to their wives. The family squabbles permitted Maggie to vicariously get back at her ex-husband to keep herself very much in control and needed. This was her insurance that she would never again be alone.

If Maggie had given up her anger and resentment at her ex-husband as well as her fear of future rejections, she may never have initiated the game. Had her sons been aware of the double messages she was sending they could have declined her invitation to play. They still have that capability and option. The solution for her daughters-in-law is to establish their priorities — accept guilt gifts, file for divorce, or tell Momma to butt out of their personal lives.

THE SECRET

Once upon a time there was a very nice bi-sexual man who really liked men better. His friends knew it and his parents knew it, but his bride-to-be did not know it. In the Fifties, closets had no doors and his parents wanted him married and respectable. The bride looked beautiful and radiant in her long white gown — *the secret* was safe.

The young man's name was Miles and his bride's name was Angela. Miles called her Angel and often told her, "You are the Angel of Beauty and Innocence." They had two children named Star and Dust. Each day Angel cleaned, cooked and sang. She didn't question Miles' love, because theirs was bright and strong. Besides, he showed NO interest in other women. Angel thought it was nice that Miles had three or four good men friends to do manly things with, while she shined her wedding silver and folded diapers. Life was indeed bountiful.

One spring evening when Miles was visiting one of his men friends, Angel received a very strange call. The voice told her to walk to Miles' friend's house and enter without knocking. Feeling uncertain and a bit frightened, she left Dust, age six, and Star, age ten, and obeyed the caller. She could not believe her eyes . . . How? Why?

Miles did not want to harm his Angel, but he was tired of secrets. He had accepted his homosexuality, and was relieved that Angel finally knew. The secret was out! Angel felt stupid, angry and shocked, but in true angel fashion turned her thoughts to the children and stayed with Miles.

The secret dispelled, Miles saw more and more of his men friends and permitted his feelings to reach the intensity he so often dreamed about. Three years later he left Angel, Star and Dust, and moved in with his lover. Angel and Miles divorced, but made a pact to keep the secret.

Miles and Peter were very happy together. They had many common interests, including their 13-year-old daughters who had known each other since infancy. One day Star told Ruth how fortunate it was that both they and their fathers were such good friends. In the name of honesty, virtue and youth, Ruth replied, "You nerd! They're gay. Our fathers aren't roommates, they're lovers."

Star felt thunder in her soul and went to seek wisdom and truth from her mother. Angel acknowledged the truth and made a pact with her to keep the secret from Dust. Star had lots of anger and questions inside her: "Why had her dad married her mom in the first place? Would she turn out to be gay? What would her friends say? Could she keep the secret? If she got married who would give her away, certainly not a fag!"

Believing her father took advantage of her mother, she set out to do him in. She refused to see him except when she wanted something, and she wanted a lot. She tested out her sexuality in many different beds. She soothed her hurt with drugs. She managed to keep the secret, but lived in hell.

This isn't a tale of sex, but rather of deceit. The lying, manipulation, and dishonesty in the interest of secrecy hurt three generations. Miles' sexuality was an embarrassment to his family, and they covered it up by promoting his marriage in an effort to save face. Miles felt ashamed and guilty for what he had done to his wife and children. Angel felt shame, shock and bitterness. Star is dealing with her pain destructively. Yet, the deceit continues as they attempt to keep the secret from Dust. How will he handle it when he finds out? He surely will!

You can tune into your family's after divorce games by using the "Game Plan" devised by John James. The procedure works like this: In your mind's eye picture each member of your family, including yourself, and ask yourself the following questions:

1. What happens over and over that leaves someone feeling bad?
2. How does it start?
3. What happens next?
4. Then what happens?
5. How does it end?
6. How do you end up feeling?
7. What do you say to yourself then?[1]

It is less than coincidental that certain family members engage in the same stereotyped arguments which result in the same bad feelings. The feeling you end up with or collect at game's end is the reason you initiated or participated in the game.

[1]Muriel James, *Transactional Analysis For Moms And Dads*, Addison-Wesley, Inc., 1974, Pg. 111-113.

8

HI,
WHAT'S YOUR SIGN?

The divorce explosion has left millions of adults and approximately one out of six children living in an almost perpetual state of transition. Anthropologists use the term *cultural lag* to describe any sweeping social change which has occurred so rapidly that the existing culture has not yet absorbed the change and established a new set of norms and guidelines. Until this occurs, those caught up in the new event are left struggling with little societal support and structure. When the culture lays down its rules and regulations, new traditions are formed.

Because of the upheaval in personal, social, sexual and marital values, traditional modes of relating are in limbo. In the not too distant past, society could handle the relatively small numbers of people who were divorcing, "living in sin," or having casual sex. Their behavior was tolerated, but frowned upon. This minority has now become a powerful social force which may soon reach parity with once traditional life styles. Society can no longer frown and look away. Provisions for alternate life styles must be made.

New relationships vary from one night stands, to casual dating, to dating one person exclusively, to living together and remarriage. In any new relationship there exists a host of myths, expectations and unanswered, as well as unasked, questions.

MYTHS AND THE NEWLY SINGLED

Movies, T.V., books, and our own fantasies tell us about happy-go-lucky ex-husbands who drink, dance and seduce their way into a new life style. They also tell us about liberated women who are free to do their own thing. Like most fables there is some truth to these notions. Nevertheless, most newly single men and women experience intense divorce distress. They are insecure personally and socially, and have difficulty with budgeting, household management and single parenting. To compound the problem, many fall victim to the myths themselves. They question and wonder why they are not feeling and doing what they have been told they *should* feel and do.

The myths lead us to believe that men get over separation and divorce distress quicker — "He won't have time to feel bad with all those women chasing him." A more realistic appraisal is that men who have not left their wives for another woman feel and act more like eunuchs than studs.

During the initial period of separation distress, both sexes are apt to withdraw and isolate as they reel from shock and sink into depression. The motivation for new relationships is the need for support and nurturance, primarily from the same sex. Relationships with the opposite sex are either avoided or superficial. During this acute phase of distress, the opposite sex is typically seen as threatening.

Once the acute stage has passed, men and women alike begin seeking out the opposite sex. However, it is not intimacy they want. Rather, it is someone, almost anyone, who will help relieve the nagging and persistent loneliness. While a man may act the part of a macho, bed-hopping bachelor, for many, sex is only a means to an end — a soft, warm body with whom he can cuddle up and sleep. Sex as a means to an end — touching — also holds true for women.

The word divorcee usually refers to a woman and carries with it a collage of negative meanings. While the negative impact of divorce has lessened, a divorced woman is often placed in one of two categories — the immoral hussy or the withered prune. If she has children and leads an active social life, she is frequently looked upon with suspicion, "Is she taking proper care of her children?" If she keeps her personal and social life confined to her home and children, she is likely to be pitied or viewed as a prude. The question becomes how to walk that fine line between social respectability, which may have little to do with morals, and human needs for social contact, personal growth and sexual satisfaction.

SEXUAL MYTHS AND THE MID YEARS

Middle-aged men report increased needs for tenderness and intimacy, a diminution of sexual aggressiveness and a tendency to become more relationship-orientated. Middle-aged women report feeling stronger, more sure of themselves and more sexually aggressive.[1] These observations fly in the face of the myths of the erotically driven, bed-hopping, macho male and the withdrawn, frightened, sexually unresponsive female.

Confrontation with one's sexuality, particularly in mid-life, is more difficult for the divorcing. The sexual attitudes and behaviors of married persons are closely linked to those of their spouse. After divorce, these attitudes and behaviors may no longer be relevant. Accordingly, a redefinition of one's sexual needs and wants becomes necessary.

Some mid-life divorcing people involve themselves in round after round of casual sex in an attempt to appear, act and feel younger. In an effort to prove that their sexual virility, desirability and responsiveness have not been affected by age, they are apt to set unrealistic performance goals which, if not met, only serve to increase sexual anxiety and decrease performance.

Dr. Martha Cleveland reports several interesting differences between the sexual attitudes of middle-aged divorcing men and women. Her observations led her to conclude that men want to prove their sexual desirability to themselves and society, while women want to prove their sexual desirability to themselves and their ex-spouse. Men want to prove their ability to perform, women their ability to attract.

---

[1]Martha Cleveland, "Divorce in the Middle Years," *Journal of Divorce*, Volume 2, No. 3, Spring 1979. Pgs. 255-262.

Some divorcing people engage in brief sexual encounters as a kind of rebellious acting out. Sex is used either as an aggressive act aimed at their ex, or toward everyone and everything. When the motivation for their sexual behavior is analyzed, these people usually come to the realization that their behavior was actually a rebellion against their own feelings of frustration, disappointment and failure.

Some women who had been sexually unresponsive and aorgasmic during marriage find that after divorce they can function perfectly normally. For the first time in their lives sex becomes exciting, satisfying, and complete. A small portion of these women involve themselves in a series of short-term sexual encounters in an unrealistic effort to make up for lost time.

While it is known and generally accepted that men often choose younger women for brief sexual encounters, lesser known, though often frowned upon, is the fact that women do also. Some men pick younger women to validate their youthfulness, while others do so to avoid the threat they feel from women their own age. Women choose younger men for similar reasons. However, there seems to be a difference between men's and women's ideas about the outcome of the relationship. A significant number of men reported expectations for a continuous, monogamous relationship with a younger woman. For the most part, women do not hold the expectation that a lasting relationship will result from these encounters.

Most mid-life divorcing people reported loneliness to be more of a problem than sex. Once the novelty and excitement of casual sex wore off, frequent one night stands tended to increase feelings of loneliness and isolation. The women in Dr. Cleveland's sample expected that sex without intimacy would be meaningless. Men, on the other hand, became confused and frightened. They were unaware of and did not understand their increased needs for tenderness, emotional closeness and intimacy.

According to Dr. Cleveland, the basic motivating forces of the sexually active, middle-aged, divorced person appear to be:

1. Rebellion
2. Validation of one's masculinity or femininity
3. The masking of past failures and hopes for another chance
4. The establishment of an intimate monogamous relationship[2]

In 1978 we conducted a survey of our column readership. The opinionaire was designed to find out what our readers thought of the opposite sex, what they believed the opposite sex wanted from them, and their own thoughts about the divorced as a group. Over 95% of the respondents were divorced and ranged in age from their mid 30's to mid 40's. The average time divorced was four and a half years.

Seventy-five per cent of our respondents wanted to remarry. Both sexes reported that the most important thing a man wants from a woman is sex. Love and companionship ranked a distant second and third. The sexes differed as to the fourth position. Men placed understanding in fourth place, whereas women said, "Men want a maid."

The slogan "We've Come a Long Way Baby" didn't hold true. The primary thing women said they wanted from a man was security. Love placed second with sex and companionship tied for third.

The thoughts the divorced had about the divorced were basically negative. Ninety-five per cent of the words and terms the divorced used to describe themselves and their fellow divorcees were derisive. Women described themselves as lonely, insecure and frightened, while men viewed them as bitter. Men didn't fare much better. Both sexes perceived them as lonely, but less so than women. Women also described their male counterparts as "fancy free playboys with sex on their minds."

In this and the following chapter, we will focus on the three primary kinds of new relationships: dating, living together and remarriage. In some instances these events follow in sequence and result in marriage. Other couples begin liv-

---

[2]Ibid., Pgs. 255-262.

ing together with very little prior knowledge of each other. It is as if they meet, disco, go to bed and move in together. Some marry impulsively out of hook love or on the rebound. Others simply date a succession of people, never getting close enough for anything other than the casual to occur.

DATING

Dating, the commonest and once the most ritualized form of interaction between two newly acquainted people, is now open to considerable questioning and uncertainty. Simple as it may have been when you were a teen or young adult, it isn't so simple when you're middle-aged, divorced after several or more years of marriage, and living in the 80's.

For the most part, the recently separated, divorced and widowed do not know how to behave on a date. You may have known what worked before, but how about now? Although you are older and supposedly more experienced and sophisticated, what do you do when the social fabric that once supported appropriate dating behavior is out of date?

How and Where?

If you have been single for a while and no longer harbor illusions of reconciliation, you are, or will soon be looking for someone to date. As you think about dating you will begin asking yourself, "Where and how do I meet someone, and if I do, then what?"

Your first answer to the question "How" is to start with you. Give yourself permission to be open and stroking. What you stroke in others is what you will receive in return. If you are cool, distant and aloof, you are signaling others to keep their distance. If you are forever fault-finding or complaining, you will attract people with the same traits and will be pushing winners away.

Next, make a list of those activities you participate in and those you think you might enjoy. Get involved in several of the latter. While participating look about and see who you would like to meet or become friendlier with. Their sex does *not* matter. What counts is their friendship. Being and feeling OK with yourself and others is the most effective way of inviting people to want to know and be with you.

If you join a singles group do not become involved in more than one whose *primary* purpose is for divorced people. These kinds of organizations can serve a valuable short-term purpose as they provide support, reassurance and strokes in times of crisis. Involving yourself in several may be self-defeating, because some tend to attract more than their share of people who use the group as a way to reinforce a "poor me" attitude out of the victim position.

Ways to meet people vary from participation in social functions, work activities, church groups, dating services, singles groups and friends. The media has picked up on the needs of the divorced to meet people. In several large metropolitan areas, radio stations have seen a market for a program to put singles in touch with each other. The format is simple. People call the station and for several minutes are put on the air, during which time they describe themselves and the type of person they would like to meet. If another listener wishes to meet the person, they call the station and are told how to contact them. As unorthodox as this sounds, its success is attested to by the continuation of this type of programming.

We again emphasize that the best way to meet others is by being an open, warm, stroking person whose very presence invites others to want to know you. If you do so, the best place to meet someone is anywhere.

What To Say

When two people begin a dating relationship, they typically experience a period of tension and tenuousness. Conversation is often choppy and faltering. Part of the choppiness is related to the question "How do I talk about me when so much of me is connected to someone else (my ex) and something else (the marital relationship)?"

The best way over this hurdle is to stay in the here and now. If you bring up your ex, come back to the present. Once you have established a history of your own, conversation will flow more rapidly, smoothly and naturally.

What To Do?

"Should I open the car door? Am I acting right? When or should I make a sexual advance?" These are but a scant few of an endless stream of questions people reentering the world of new relationships ask. The answers depend on specific people in specific situations. Once you get to know the person you will develop a feel for his interests, wants and attitudes. Their mode of dress, way of speaking, and favorite topics of conversation will clue you in to their likes, dislikes, and expectations.

Hook Love

After a long, dry spell of stroke deprivation, interaction with a warm stroking person of the opposite sex can invite you to feel wanted, desired and worthwhile. The stroking, combined with that intangible "attraction for" can make you vibrate with joy and excitement. You begin to feel and act like an adolescent with a terminal case of the "I can't live without you's."

This intense feeling of personal and physical attraction is called "Hook Love." Hook love is tremendously exciting, yet seldom lasts for more than four to six months. During this period, one's Adult is so contaminated by joy and excitement that the "loved one" is idealized and placed on an unrealistic pedestal. As more Adult data is permitted into the perception, the loved one is seen more realistically. When this occurs, the relationship can rupture or develop into a lasting, intimate love relationship. The danger with Hook Love is that some people impulsively marry before they engage their Adult.

Dating and Kids

Unless a parent has an exclusive dating relationship, it is advisable that they not permit the various new people in their life to become too closely involved with their children. Making and breaking relationships is tough enough on adults, let alone children who have already experienced several traumatic losses.

Since children often view their parent's dates as threats, don't be surprised if your reception, even as a casual date, is less than friendly. Should you date their parent frequently and see the children often, resist the temptation to discipline. Until you have established a specific role in their lives and have the backing of their parent, you are still an intruder — a potential mother/father snatcher. If you don't like children, don't like his/her children, or don't wish to raise another person's child, think long and hard about the relationship.

DATING GAMES

PIT STOP

Lila's parents were poor, and as a child she learned how to scrape and scramble in order to survive. Not too many months ago she muttered, "I kicked out my lazy, no good husband and now I have to take care of my kid and save enough bread for a divorce." A tenth grade education left her with few good occupational choices, so she took a job as a clerk on the 3-11 P.M. shift at one of the local hospitals.

After several weeks on the job, the night shift threw a party. Impressed with the people, the host's apartment, and what to her was affluence, she let herself go and drank too much. Sometime during the evening Jim was elected to see her safely home.

Jim, a recently separated doctor, didn't feel like partying, but out of loneliness let himself be persuaded to attend. Although he didn't know Lila, he agreed to take her home, for it was a perfect opportunity to graciously escape from an uncomfortable situation. Since Lila lived across town, he decided to take her to his apartment, pour some coffee down her and drive her back to her car. When they arrived, she passed out on the sofa. As he watched her sleeping, he felt surprised at how good it felt just to have another warm body in the apartment. Her very presence seemed to add warmth to his stark environment, so he let her stay the rest of the night. Over breakfast the next morning, each discovered the other was separated, uninvolved, and except for work, kept themselves isolated. With the proper thank-yous and good-byes, they went their separate ways.

Lila couldn't get Jim out of her thoughts. He had been so gentle and kind. She had never before experienced this in a man. She began watching for Jim at the hospital, but never saw him. One evening just before the end of her shift, she summoned up her courage and called him to see if it would be all right to stop by and say hello. Lila made her first Pit Stop! Arriving at 11:30 P.M., in bed by midnight, and on her way home by 3:00 A.M. became their routine.

As a teenager Jim had been shy and awkward with girls. He never really learned how to start or end a relationship. He either let the girl make the first move or waited for something to happen. His first "sweetheart," whom he later married, made the first move. She even proposed. After his separation, he hated the idea of dating and "going on the hunt." Lila made it easy. She found him, pursued him and listened, touched and made love, with no strings.

In the beginning, Jim was very excited by Lila's earthiness and sensuality. He was also taken by her lack of sophistication, which in some ways bordered on a childlike naiveté. She loved to pamper him, do for him, and make love to him. Her only want was that he be gentle with her. Her lack of complexity and willingness to give made her Pit Stops a very important and pleasurable part of Jim's life.

From the start Jim was very clear with Lila, "No public appearances until the divorce and settlement are all tied up in a nice legal knot." Lila agreed and Pit Stop continued nonstop for several months. On the surface this appeared to be a rational Adult decision. In reality, being seen with another woman would not have jeopardized Jim's position vis-á-vis the divorce. The agreement was Jim's Con. Lila's acceptance came out of her Gimmick or desire to be with her dream man — good-looking, educated and financially secure.

As the months rolled by, feeling hemmed in and yearning for some excitement, Lila nagged Jim for an occasional night out. Although Jim held her to the agreement, he eventually came to the realization that he simply did not want to be seen with her in public. She was pretty, but uneducated. She was beneath his social standing and couldn't hold her own with his friends and colleagues. Except for sex they had nothing in common. In short, he was embarrassed to be seen with her. Nevertheless, he didn't want to give up her Pit Stops.

Lila was falling in love with Jim. She was so caught up in her fantasy that he would marry her that she never bothered to put two and two together. Why, for example, would he keep her a secret from his closest friends? Surely, they wouldn't tell his wife. Instead, she held onto her belief that if he were "free" they would be out with his friends, having a good time and planning their marriage.

The day Jim's attorney called and told him the divorce was final, he was jolted by two disparate feelings — relief that the ordeal of the divorce was over and concern over what he was going to do with Lila. At that point he pulled the Switch on Lila. He kept the news a secret.

He continued to enjoy her nightly Pit Stops, while looking for someone more appropriate during the day. When he found a girl more in keeping with his background and status, he gradually closed down the "pit" with excuses like, "I had a hard day today," "I have to be in the operating room at 6:30 A.M.," "I've got a medical society meeting tonight." Several times he even had a buddy play "host" to Lila while he was supposedly out on an emergency.

When Lila finally let Jim's message seep through her fantasy, she made an unscheduled Pit Stop and unleashed her anger at him. As she slammed the door behind her, Jim breathed a guilty sigh of relief. Driving home she collected her Payoff, "You stupid fool, you should have known you weren't *good enough* for a doctor."

At a staff cocktail party, Jim heard that Lila was playing Pit Stop with a salesman. He silently felt sorry for her, finished his glass of champagne and rejoined the group.

IODINE

Molly carried on Florence Nightingale's tradition in good, after-divorce fashion. Her last three lovers came staggering out of divorce court into her waiting arms. Molly listened, nurtured, and cared for them. After number three made his exit, she began asking herself why the men in her life picked up and left just when she felt their relationship was becoming intimate and they were getting back on their personal, social and financial feet.

Molly was divorced herself and knew how it felt to be confused, alone and hurt. Being the possessor of a gigantic Nurturing Parent, she joined several organizations whose primary purpose for existing was divorce and its problems. By involving herself in these organizations she was able to dispense her bandages and iodine, and look for a man. Her warm, empathetic manner, her home-cooked meals, and the fact that her time and bed were accessible, drew these wounded men to her. Molly's problem was not attracting, but rather, sustaining a relationship.

When we first met Molly, her anger, hurt and confusion were developing into a full-blown depression. After only a few sessions she became aware that her overgrown Nurturing Parent had contaminated her Adult. She learned that she had joined these organizations out of an exaggerated need to be needed, and that by choosing the walking wounded, who were not capable of sustaining a lasting relationship, she was signaling, "Come home to momma *until* you get well." These men picked up on her signals and did just that. When she became less depressed we asked, "Do you have First Aid Station written on your front door?" She responded with a smile and a new decision not to date a man who had been divorced less than six months. Molly retired her first aid kit.

Molly's Con was, "Let me bandage your wounds." Her ulterior motive was, "I want a permanent love relationship." The Gimmick her Con hooked into was these men's feelings of hurt, loneliness and helplessness. They responded by permitting her to take them under her wing. After a month or two of playing nurse and patient, she pulled the Switch by attempting to trade in her nurse's cap for a bridal veil. Their wounds healed, no longer in need of a nurse and not wanting to get married, they left. Molly's Payoff was to feel betrayed and martyred, "After all I've done for you."

PLASTIC SURGERY

Martha was in her late 40's when she divorced after spending the last 22 years as a mother and housewife. Nonetheless, she handled the legal and practical aspects of the divorce amazingly well. Her college degree made entry in the job market easier, and by all appearances it seemed as if she had it all together. Appearances aside, her personal life was in a shambles.

Her Parent tapes on how an unmarried woman should act weighed so heavily on her that she shut herself off from the here and now, particularly when it came to men. She had been reared to believe "nice ladies" don't approach or speak to strange men unless properly introduced, were never to go out alone for the evening, and were to be married and center their lives around a man. Her tapes told her that women who worked outside the home were of lower social standing. Martha was also confused and upset over her sexual urges. Being a proper lady, she never discussed these feelings with other divorced women and assumed that single women her age simply stopped being sexual. Nevertheless, much of her time was spent fighting back erotic thoughts and sexual feelings.

Unaware that her outdated tapes were cutting off her chances to create a new life which included fun, dating and sex if she wished, she zeroed in on her looks as the reason for her unhappiness. She likened the skin under her eyes to supermarket bags, saw the traces of crows feet as deep crevices, and was appalled that her once pert breasts were beginning that inevitable downward plunge. She began hating her body and concluded that the way to a happier life was through plastic surgery.

Martha wasn't totally off base. Self-esteem is related to physical appearance. However, she was connng herself by blaming her appearance for her difficulties and viewing surgery as the sole remedy. Dipping into her savings, she had a face life and breast augmentation. Within a month the only visible traces of her miracle cure were a few small bruises.

Martha waited and waited for her new life to begin. Nothing happened! Out of desperation she attended a workshop for the divorced. She looked beautiful, poised and *closed*. As the participants discussed their ideas and feelings about changing social standards, particularly as related to new relationships and sex, she internally protested, "Nice ladies don't act like that." When the workshop turned its attention to "How to meet people," all she permitted herself to think was, "I would never go to any of those places unescorted." If a woman brought up a subject that contradicted one of Martha's Parent tapes, she silently discounted the person and withdrew even further into her shell. As if her tapes hadn't been challenged sufficiently for one day, the group embarked upon a series of stroking exercises. Martha refused to recognize her inability to give genuine strokes at either the verbal or physical level. It became clear to everyone but her that she needed an ego state lift more than a face lift.

Solutions for Martha are readily available. Her first task is to engage her Adult in order to evaluate and update her Parent tapes. She must then learn to diminish her Critical Parent and develop her Nurturing Parent and Free Child. Until she learns to stroke herself and others, she will continue to withdraw and cut herself off from new relationships, be they with men or women.

Plastic surgery is an example of an internally played, single-handed game. Despite Martha's surgery, her life remained the same because she stayed in her Adapted Child and lived by outdated Parent tapes. Her concern over her physical appearance and belief that the royal road to happiness was through surgery was her Con.

DON'T RUFFLE HER ANGEL FEATHERS

Janet and Bob had an exclusive dating relationship for over two years. Janet, custodial parent of two children, and Bob, non-custodial parent of three children, kept in close touch with their ex's because of the children. They had planned on marrying, but at the moment their relationship was going down the drain. According to Janet the bulk of their problems were over how Bob dealt with his ex.

"A couple of months ago as we were leaving for dinner, Bob's ex called complaining about money and asking for another increase in child support. That conversation started our evening off with a bang. During the first half of dinner I listened to him complain about how poorly his ex managed her finances and that she was forever trying to get more money out of him. When I agreed, he turned on me. I spent the rest of dinner listening to him defend her. As if I didn't already know, he lectured me on the enormous cost of raising children in today's inflationary economy. Was I ever furious! By the time the check arrived he was actually feeling guilty over spending money at a restaurant while his poor ex-wife was about to go to the poor house. We may as well have invited *her*, since that's all he talked about all evening. As usual he increased the amount of support. That wasn't the only increase. He also stepped up his complaining!

Not long after that episode, she called and told him there was more to parenting than sending money. She said she couldn't keep leaving work to take the youngest to soccer practice, the middle one to the orthodontist and the eldest to driving school. So, if he wanted a soccer player whose brother had straight teeth and whose sister could drive, he would have to do it.

Bob ranted and raved over a custodial parent's responsibilities. 'She had the gall to tell me what I had to do without even discussing it.' He couldn't see how he could pay the bills *and* take off work. I agreed with some of his points and made several suggestions including that he consider seeking custody.

The worm turned, and as usual, on me, not her! For the next 30 minutes I got a lecture on how tough things are for her, what a good mother she is, and while she may seem hard and bitchy that's the way she honestly views things. They eventually worked things out — he did 50% and paid for 100%.

The straw that broke the camel's back came on one of those few evenings my children were away and Bob stayed over. The next day she called and chewed him out because she hadn't been able to get a hold of him and in the event of an emergency she couldn't have reached him. She also threw in that the kids knew he was sleeping with *that* woman. As usual, he was stomping mad.

In an attempt to support him, I pointed out that if she knew he was at my house she would have been able to reach him. I should have known better! He took up for her saying how embarrassing it would have been for her to call my house. That did it! Not only is it none of her damn business where he is 24 hours a day, I'm tired of him jumping all over my case every time I agree how bitchy she is. He acts as if she's an angel and I ruffled her feathers."

If you examine Janet's comments, it is evident that Bob is at the helm. While on the surface it appears that he is the one that's being dumped on, in reality, he has set it up to be in control of two women who are providing him with abundant sources of strokes, both positive and negative.

By refusing to set firm limits for his ex and acceding to her demands, he keeps her dependent on him — power strokes. His complaints to Janet and her nurturing strokes set him up to be the good guy who is doing his best to satisfy the insatiable and sometimes inappropriate demands of his ex.

Bob's Con is, "What a demanding bitch my ex-wife is." His ulterior motive is, "See how powerful I am." Janet's Gimmick is to play rescuer. Bob's Switch is to turn on Janet and persecute her when she agrees with him. His Payoff is to feel needed yet victimized by his ex wife, and misunderstood by Janet. Janet's Payoff is to feel angry, frustrated and cornered. After all, how can you fault a guy who is providing for his children?

As long as Bob permits his ex-wife to make demands and he plays "poor me" with Janet, he keeps the strokes forthcoming. If Janet exits, he can increase the complexity of the game and the frequency of strokes with the next woman he dates by complaining about both his ex-wife and Janet.

Bob could have cut the game off at its inception had he not had the need to maintain his power base with his ex and set firm limits as to what he would and would not do. He could have avoided gaming with Janet had he not reported to her. Janet could have cut through the game transaction by refusing to defend Bob, which resulted in a game of "Yes, But Don't Ruffle Her Angel Feathers." The fact that each time she agreed with him and offered a solution he turned on her should have told her that Bob was attempting to remain in his *contrived* victim position as opposed to seeking a real solution. The rule of thumb in a game of, "Yes, But . . ." is to stop offering solutions after three "Yes, buts."

DAD CATCHER

Eight-year-old Meg adored her father and in her eyes he could do no wrong. Her adulation was of such magnitude that her perception of him as a person, man and father was idealized and distorted. Watching the two of them together reminded one of a puppy dog following alongside its master.

Her dad's steady girl, Dee, was 23 and almost 15 years her Father's junior. Dee also followed him around like a puppy dog. Dee and Meg's dad were together so much of the time that she and Meg saw a lot of each other. Togetherness increased as Dee accepted many of the parental tasks and functions Troy gave her.

Meg accepted Dee's intrusions with considerable ambivalence. Although she disliked having to share her father, her distorted perceptions forged yet another misperception, "Daddy's so busy he has Dee take care of me." Meg's idealization of and fear of losing her father prevented her from openly expressing her anger at him for his absences, and at Dee for trespassing on what she considered her territory.

Dee was quite content with the scene. She liked Troy, his house, his condominium in Vail, his sports car, his sailboat and what she figured were several substantial bank accounts. The only thing she wasn't content with was the snail's pace at which she and Troy were approaching the altar. She wanted to speed up the pace! After careful thought and consideration the solution became clear and simple — Meg.

Dee attempted to become Meg's friend and confidante. She took her places, bought her all sorts of nice gifts, and kept telling her how much she loved her father. Whenever the three of them did anything together, Dee would invariably recount to Meg the fun events of the preceding day, never failing to mention all the good times *they* could have together if she and her dad were married.

Dee's plan backfired. The more she spoke to Meg of marriage and the greater the pressure she exerted on her to play matchmaker, the angrier Meg became. Even at eight, she was able to see the gold digger in Dee. Meg became determined to protect her father from this menace. She also sensed that if her father married Dee, she would be displaced.

Angry and threatened, Meg told her mother what was happening. Mom came to the rescue by calling Troy and telling him how Dee was using Meg and how miserable Meg felt. It didn't take long before Dee was out the door. Mom's call was not purely altruistic. She was still angry at Troy for divorcing her and couldn't stand the idea of his dating those young "chicks."

This dating relationship turned into a complicated four-handed game with each party acting out their own Cons and Gimmicks. Troy used Dee as a surrogate mother and babysitter. Dee accepted the role in order to manipulate Meg into helping her to the altar. Mom used Meg's unhappiness as her entree to get back at Troy. Meg told on Dee in an attempt to keep her favored place with her father.

Until Troy meets his daughter's needs for a father, Meg feels valued as a daughter, and Troy and his ex-wife give up their anger and bad feelings toward one another, the games will continue.

GOLD DIGGER

Nick, a well-to-do manufacturer's representative, has been divorced eight years, and has yet to understand or forgive his ex-wife for divorcing him. His last in a lengthy series of short-lived relationships was with Dina, a sophisticated and successful businesswoman who enjoys the finer things in life.

On their first date Nick took Dina to dinner at an exclusive restaurant. He nearly turned green when he saw the check, $95, not including tip. While waiting for the parking attendant to bring his car around, he told her he could not afford these kinds of evenings again. On their second date Nick asked her to choose the restaurant. Remembering his comments about money she chose a less expensive restaurant, but one which still fit her tastes. Nick reacted angrily, exclaiming that it was too expensive, and chose one himself.

Sensitized to Nick's concerns over money she ordered

sensibly, but nonetheless was determined not to eat sirloin burger. As Nick recalculated the check and computed the tax, Dina again saw that look of anger and disdain on his face. From the time and energy he consumed in figuring the tip, one might have thought he was the Chairman of the Federal Reserve attempting to curb inflation by determining the appropriate rate of interest. Dina decided she had had enough. At the end of the evening she told Nick she no longer wished to see him. When pressed for her reasons, she was kind but truthful. She told him that she was uncomfortable with his attitudes and behavior about money and that when they were out he acted as though she were trying to bankrupt him. Nick responded angrily and lectured her about women's disregard for and irresponsibility with money.

Nick's tirade was but one of a series he had given to many other women, particularly his ex-wife, whom he considered an irresponsible spendthrift. Exploration of Nick's early life revealed that his money games were directly related to a lack of emotional security and the very real threat of poverty he faced as a child. During middle childhood his mother became manic-depressive. During her manic phases she became extremely impulsive, spent money foolishly and wrote bad checks. When she became depressed, she often threatened suicide and on two occasions made unsuccessful, though serious attempts. The cost of psychiatric care was staggering.

For Nick, money symbolized security, and women, insecurity. Money became his way of protecting himself against loss, material or personal. However, this line of defense only served to make his worst fears come true as his attitudes and behavior with money drove his wife and others away from him. As a result he felt even less secure and became tighter. The circle was never-ending.

In therapy Nick became aware of how his early family experiences molded his childhood decisions and present behaviors with money. He learned to use money for him, not against him.

THE GIG

Sally and her eleven-year-old daughter Kim were planning to spend their vacation with Sally's parents who lived in a small New England tourist town. Visiting her parents was always a joy, for the town held special meaning for her — so much so that she was very possessive of it. Even when she and Joe were married, she was selective about whom she invited to her little Shangri-La.

The day before leaving, Kim excitedly announced that her Dad and his girlfriend were going to fly up to Rockford to visit her and her grandparents. Kim babbled on and on about all the wonderful things she and her Dad were going to do. Sally was beside herself. Joe hadn't seen or spoken to her parents in the two years since their divorce and to come uninvited with a girlfriend was absurd. "Over my dead body," she thought.

Sally spent a sleepless night mulling over the possibilities. "Why would he want to come? Can I stop him? Why is he bringing a girlfriend? He wouldn't dare bring *her* to my parents' home, but then he just might. What will my family say?"

Arriving angry and exhausted, she immediately told her parents about Joe's plans. Her mom quietly said, "Joe is coming to show off for us." Her dad, a small aging man, stated matter of factly, "If he brings another woman here, I'll throw him off the property." For Kim's benefit it was agreed that Joe could visit so long as he came alone and that Kim could spend the day in town with him.

The big day came and Joe arrived at the house alone. Despite the fact that he was treated congenially, the air was filled with tension and awkwardness. His clothing and jewelry reeked of success, but no one inquired about this aspect of his life. After an hour or so he told Kim he had to leave because he couldn't leave his girlfriend alone at the motel. Joe never called Kim back. In fact, no even knew when he left. Kim stayed on pins and needles waiting for a call that never came.

Joe was furious when Sally asked for a divorce. He felt rejected and abandoned and ever since the divorce played get back AT. At every opportunity he gigged her with his business successes, new possessions and young girlfriends. A 1300 mile trip with a girlfriend to *her* town for an hour's visit and then to run out on Kim was one gig Sally could hardly ignore. Joe made his point, "I have the time and money to come all the way here just for an hour . . . look at what you gave up."

Joe's plan wasn't entirely successful. Sally's parents didn't bite the hook by centering the conversation around Joe and his success. Sally was able to keep her feelings in check because of her parents' Adult explanation as to the real meaning of Joe's visit and their insight that the girlfriend was merely a ploy used in an attempt to incite Sally.

Joe's Con was telling Kim he was coming to Rockford to be with her and to visit his ex-in-laws. The ulterior motive was, "I'll show everyone what you gave up." Sally's Gimmick was her anger at Joe, and viewing Rockford as her exclusive territory. Joe's Switch was his brief visit, and leaving without so much as a goodbye. His Payoff was a vengeful, "I showed them." Sally's Payoff was anger for the way he treated Kim, feeling intruded upon, and wondering when he would strike again. Kim, like the girlfriend, was a pawn in Joe's game plan. She was left feeling hurt and abandoned.

Sally could have nipped the game in the bud by using her Adult to figure out the purpose of Joe's visit. While she may have been unable to prevent his trip, she would not have lost a night's sleep or turned herself into an emotional wreck waiting for his next move.

MAKE BELIEVE

Gena and Cliff met while each was going through a painful divorce. The strain, heartache and loss left each one's stroke reserve depleted. This pushed them all too quickly into an exclusive relationship. The legal realities of Cliff's divorce precluded that he be seen in public with a woman, so they spent almost all of their time alone and clinging to each other in his apartment.

Insulated from the outside world they shared their fears, bodies, and the anguish of their divorce experiences. As the weeks passed and their contact with others diminished, they became increasingly attached to and dependent upon one another. They alternated between taking care of and nurturing each other's wounds and uncertainties. Theirs was a Child-Child/Nurturing Parent-Child relationship. Before they realized it they had slipped into an exclusive relationship.

Being in hook love, they began living with each other shortly after their respective divorces. As they unhooked from their ex-spouses and the marital relationships, they began to require less and less of what the other had been providing. As a result the relationship began showing signs of stress as each wished, wanted, and sometimes demanded something different from the other. Seldom was it forthcoming. Because their relationship was founded on Child fears and Nurturing Parent strokes, little time was spent exploring and learning about the other parts of their personalities. In many ways they were strangers.

The basis upon which they originally formed their relationship was becoming less and less viable as each developed a new sense of self along with altered needs, wants and expectations for themselves, the other and the relationship. When they first met, their identities were fractured, their separation distress intense and their stroke reserve so low that they viewed each other through narrow peepholes. As they felt more sure of themselves, and with renewed confidence, their fields of vision widened. These altered perceptions and the ability to function effectively as single people were such that they found themselves emotionally attached to someone with whom they no longer fit. Although each secretly knew the relationship was unworkable, the prospect of another emotional loss was overwhelming. They stuck it out for several more months before breaking up. This loss was nearly as painful as their divorces.

Gena and Cliff's game of Make Believe was, in large part, a product of separation distress. Each was hurting and made believe the other could take away the pain. Each was alone and made believe the other could take away the loneliness. Each was struggling to develop a new sense of self and made believe the other could solidify their identity. Neither really knew the other, yet made believe they did. Both were reacting to realistic crises, and they grasped onto one another as though they were life preservers. Their Adult ego states were contaminated, and therefore their ability to think and evaluate impaired.

The hurt and loss they caused each other could have been avoided had they not gotten involved so quickly. Recently separated and divorced persons should give themselves time to reidentify themselves and to learn how to be on their own once again. We believe, and the data bears this out, that remarrying one year or less after divorce carries an inordinate risk. We also believe that the establishment of an exclusive dating relationship or living together arrangement should not occur until one has forged a new and independent concept of self and personal identity.

None of us is above playing games before marriage, during marriage or after divorce. After divorce games are based on a need for strokes, a fractured identity, unconscious childhood decisions and an emotional attachment to an exspouse. The following checklist will help you to clarify where you are and to curtail or even avoid after divorce games.

Ask Yourself the Following:

1. Am I attempting to live up to a myth? If so, what is the myth?
2. Is my positive stroke reserve low? Do I know how to give and get positive strokes?
3. Will I find ways to meet new people?
4. What kinds of words and terms do I use to describe me, a divorced person?
5. Do I see my single status as a permanent or transient state?

6. Do I wish to be in a traditional or liberated role? Are these roles the same in business, social and dating situations?

7. Have I explained to my children that I will be dating and that every person I see is not a potential marriage partner? Are my children in competition with my dates for my time and attention?

8. What are my expectations of the opposite sex? Are they updated or are they outdated?

9. What do I want out of a dating relationship?

10. Would I have sex in order to lie next to a warm body?

11. Do I need another person in order to feel whole?

12. Do I spend a lot of time talking about my ex-spouse?

13. Am I unhooked from my ex-spouse sufficiently so that I can fully give of myself in a new relationship?

14. Did I enter into an exclusive relationship too soon after my divorce?

15. Am I in hook love? If so, what are the possible dangers?

16. Can I identify the marriage games that I have continued to play after divorce?

17. Which of the games in this chapter am I most likely to play?

―――――――――――――――――― **9**―

MARRIAGE-GO-ROUND

LIVING TOGETHER

If you are, or are planning on, living with someone and don't believe you need that "piece of paper" to legitimize your love and the relationship, you had better put something in writing that states your rights, responsibilities and liabilities. Sound unromantic and crass? Maybe so, but what's so romantic about being taken to court by an ex-roommate who claims to own half the assets accumulated during the period you shared the same bed? What's so romantic about being splashed through the media like Lee Marvin and Michelle Triola Marvin? Living together without some sort of written agreement leaves both parties vulnerable and unprotected if and when they break up.

The U.S. Census Bureau reported that the number of non-married couples sharing a household has increased 800% in the last fifteen years and 100% in the last five years. In the one year period between 1977 and 1978 the number of non-married couples living together increased from 957,000 to 1,137,000. In 1978 these couples accounted for 2.3% of all coupled households in the United States. The 272,000 unmarried couples with children present in the home constituted 5% of the 5.7 million single parent households in the U.S.[1]

―――――――――――
[1]*Population Bulletin*, Vol. 32, No. 5, Feb. 1979.

The number of people being taken to court by an ex-lover is increasing, and Marvin vs. Marvin is only the tip of a massive socio-legal iceberg. The issues at stake are more than the obvious ones of alimony, child support and a property settlement. Social security benefits, tax liabilities, pensions, cash value and death benefits of life insurance policies, along with rights of inheritance, are additional matters whose disposition requires a document which states who is what to whom, and who has rights to what. If you don't make these decisions ahead of time, rest assured someone else will.

In far too many instances couples *slide* into a living together arrangement. As a couple spends more and more time together, clothing and other personal effects are left at the other's residence. Little by little they co-mingle belongings and make joint purchases. Getting up early to drive "home," bathe and dress for work becomes an inconvenience. It is only a matter of time before they decide they are, for all intents and purposes, living together and give up an unused apartment.

Decisions to live together based upon this or a similar set of circumstances are not decisions about people, relationships or commitments. They have more to do with convenience, logistics, and what for the moment feels good. Therefore, it is not surprising that many people, especially the young, have numerous, short-lived, living together experiences. It is as if they go from one "feel good" convenience to another.

Living together arrangements involving children seem to be given greater forethought and consideration. There have been few good studies on the effects of living together on children. Doctors Kristen Rosenthal and Harry Keshet surveyed 127 divorced fathers in the Boston area.[2] The men in their sample ranged in age from 27 to 45, were predominantly white, middle class, well educated and separated for at least one year. Custody arrangments ranged from occasional visitation to being the custody parent. None of the men had remarried and 15 were living with a lover. Most of the women were of similar backgrounds, considerably younger than the men, and few had children of their own.

---

[2]Kristine M. Rosenthal and Harry F. Keshet, "The Not-Quite Stepmother," *Psychology Today*, July 1978.

During the first year of separation, fathers in the Rosenthal-Keshet study dated many women and their children met a number of them, though quite casually. After the first year, dating habits changed as the men began dating one woman at a time. For the most part the couples did not attempt to form many mutual bonds or obligations and the relationship remained casual and readily terminated. Sensing the tenuousness of the new adult to adult relationship, oftentimes the children attempted to do away with the intruder who threatened their bond with the natural parent. While the children attempted to keep distance between their father and his new lover, the men also tended to use the children as an excuse to keep from becoming too involved.

If the couple saw each other frequently enough, mutual interests, activities, friendships and routines developed. As a result the children began to expect the lover's presence and habitual patterns of living were created. Most of the couples saw each other four to six months before the woman stayed overnight with her lover's children present. Nevertheless, three-fourths of the men experienced anxiety over exposing their children to their sex lives.

Once a coalition between father, children and lover is formed, each must negotiate for his own place, rights and wants. When it came to negotiating power, more often than not, the woman was low man on the totem pole. If she hadn't established a specific place and role function within the family, her power was limited.

The study highlighted the fact that fathers often behaved in a way to maintain distance between their lovers and their children. Fathers rationalized this behavior by stating that they were protecting their children from another potentially painful emotional separation. They neglected to say, possibly because it was unconscious, that their behavior also protected them from the threat of having to share the already divided loyalties of their children with yet another adult.

Nonetheless, closeness can and does develop between the new woman and the children. The less a father mediated and controlled the lover-child relationship, the greater the degree of closeness. The presence of an independent relationship between lover and children signaled the growth of a new family unit. One sign of this coming together was that fathers felt free, in their children's presence, to express anger or affection toward their lovers.

An ex-spouse, though physically absent, was still a very real and often powerful force within the new family unit. Much of what the ex says, does and thinks affects the lover's life. In many ways the lover has limited say over events in the home.

In order to make a living together arrangement work, it is urgent that the new family member, the lover, have a well-defined role and status. He/she must know where he/she stands with the living partner as well as with the children. The children, particularly if they are adolescents, should know without question how their custody parent feels about the new adult in the household as well as their parent's expectations and demands about how they should respond to the lover. This structure serves a protective function as it defines rights, expectations and responsibilities for all.

An excellent way of defining role functions and creating structure is through the use of a personal relationship contract. The purpose of the contract is to make attitudes and expectations explicit. A contract makes the implicit explicit. No second guessing, no mind reading and no hedging because, "I didn't know," or "I wasn't sure."

Armed with a personal relationship contract, a non-married couple knows what to expect and what not to expect, what to count on and what not to count on, where personal time, space and money begins, ends and is co-mingled. The contract helps to prevent the legal and financial pitfalls previously discussed.

NO HOT WATER

Olivia and John were born in the early 1940's, and like most children of that era accepted their parents' teachings with little hesitation. The social climate in which they grew up was, relative to the mid 60's and 70's, placid — no student protests, no rioting in the streets and the good guys wore white hats. Like Tevye in *Fiddler On The Roof,* they had their traditions.

Wary of being an old maid, Olivia married her first husband when she was nineteen. John, her lover, waited until he was twenty-one. Their marriages lasted fourteen and fifteen years respectively. Each came out of the divorce emotionally spent and feeling guilty over the failure — marriage is forever.

Shortly before their divorces became final, they met and quickly established an exclusive dating relationship. Soon after their divorces, they entered into a semi-living together relationship, resisting a full-time arrangement because of Olivia's children. Many a night John snuck into her bed after the kids were asleep only to escape at dawn before they awoke.

This bit of deception served a threefold purpose. It lent an added bit of excitement to their already hot romance, was consistent with their Parent tapes about keeping sex out of their children's lives, and gave them an opportunity to challenge and rebel against their upbringing. In many ways they were acting and feeling like a couple of teenagers whose parents said "No!"

Their attempts at deception didn't elude the sharp eyes and ears of Olivia's two preteens. With childlike audacity and an updated perception of the world of interpersonal relationships and life styles, they informed Olivia that they knew all about her late night escapades. With permission granted, semi became full time.

After John settled in, it was decided that he would make a financial contribution to the household, would help Olivia with household chores, would accept some responsibility for her children, and would lend a hand in planning their social lives. However, such specifics as how much money and when, what chores and how often, and what responsibilities for the kids were never discussed, let alone agreed upon. Considering the complexities of running a two-family household, they hadn't even scratched the surface of formulating a workable living together arrangement. In effect, they slid into a new life style with traditional values and expectations.

With kids consenting, housekeeping set up, and John and Olivia glowing, the months flew by. *Patterns of living and*

*relating seemed to establish themselves as if they were inde-
pendent of the people living them.*

Discontent first surfaced with Olivia. While she enjoyed
keeping house, she felt that John was taking advantage of
her. They weren't married, yet she felt that John expected her
to treat him as though they were. He got up in the morning
and ate the breakfast she prepared, came home from work
and ate the dinner she cooked, and then went off to the T.V.
and couch to nap while she cleaned the kitchen. Hadn't they
agreed that he would help with the household chores, and
weren't shopping, cooking, and washing dishes household
chores?

Olivia was also upset over the financial arrangement.
One week he might hand her $50 and the next week it might
be $150. She never knew what to count on nor when it was
forthcoming. She didn't like to ask for money, but it was
becoming a necessity. She began feeling like a hostess with a
permanent guest. The weekends became increasingly irritat-
ing. John seldom planned ahead or made reservations for
dinner, the theater or a racquetball court. That also had
become her responsibility.

Surveying her situation, she couldn't believe that a year
and a half had passed. As she became more and more in
touch with her resentments, she realized that she had never
really been single. She had gone from her parents, to her husband, to a quasi-marriage with John. Questions kept running
through her head, "What are my commitments? Should I stay
with John? If I break if off, how do I do it?"

From John's perspective, things weren't all roses either.
He worked hard, helped support the family, didn't run around
on Olivia, and yet she was always on his back complaining
about something. Since the house wasn't his and they weren't
married, he wasn't sure how, when or even if he should discipline her children. He hadn't had a hot shower in weeks since
Olivia let the kids waste all the hot water. That wasn't their only wasteful habit. The T.V., stereo and lights were constantly
left on. He resented her daily complaints about his hair in the
bathtub. He tried to clean it up, but it wasn't his fault that he
was losing his hair. Besides, it wasn't as bad as her smelly
ashtrays.

Not unlike Olivia, John was also having second thoughts. He didn't like his plight, yet he didn't want to give her up. He had been through one crisis, his divorce, and didn't wish to experience another. Still, he knew that they couldn't go on like this. He mulled their problems over, asking himself how they could work out their differences when they were in an almost constant state of disagreement. He recalled how it was when they first met and how anxious he was to be with her . . . what had happened?

Olivia and John didn't look before they "slid," and as a result potential games were set up around money, her children and role functions. Whether conflict arose over hot water, John's cooking, or hair in the bathtub, the crux of their difficulties lay in the fact that they entered into a living together relationship with ill-defined objectives, methods and commitments. Because they had not agreed upon explicit role functions, each tended to fall back upon traditional ways of behaving.

Was Olivia a surrogate wife, lover or business partner? Was John a surrogate husband, lover or boarder? Was living together a convenient solution to their after divorce distress and loneliness? Had they simply been caught up in hook love? Since they never addressed themselves to these questions, they were unable to look at the true nature and motives for their relationship, let alone correct them. From the beginning they were bound for failure.

Olivia and John could have maximized the probability of a successful non-marital partnership by entering into a personal relationship contract. The very act of working through and negotiating such an agreement would have forced them to look at, discuss and decide upon a host of issues, expectations and questions. Here is a sampling of the more basic issues:

1. What are my needs, wants and expectations from the other? To what extent is he/she willing to meet them?

2. What does my lover need, want and expect from me? To what extent am I willing to meet these expectations?

3. If children are present in the household, what is the new person's role?

4. How will we deal with friends, relatives and neighbors?

5. How will household duties be handled? This includes decisions about who does what and when.

6. Exactly how and in what manner will financial matters be handled?

7. What possessions are mine, yours and ours?

8. How will the relationship be ended? It is important that couples agree upon a way to separate without adding additional burdens to an already painful situation. This is particularly important because, unlike marriage, people leaving a living together arrangement do not have traditional sources of support. Legalized marriage and divorce are institutionalized in that they are part and parcel of a package of social rites and rituals. Separation and divorce elicit helping behavior from others. For the most part, this is absent in a living together arrangement.

If you live together without thinking through these issues, you are setting yourself up for games. In John and Olivia's case their Con was "I love you." Their Gimmick was silent and implied needs and expectations. The Switch occurred when each said what they really wanted. People can live together successfully, but it takes skill, honesty and clarity of purpose and intentions.

I NOW PRONOUNCE YOU MAN AND WIFE

Julie and Gordon moved in together soon after Julie graduated with her Ph.D. and Gordon passed the Bar exam. June was a milestone for both of them. Hard, self-disciplined years in school finally over, their futures seemed bright and assured. Gordon joined a law firm as a junior partner and Julie accepted a position on the staff of Memorial Research Center.

Aside from their careers, theirs was a relationship of creativity, vibrancy and equality. Julie's water colors and

Gordon's plants gave their new apartment a very special personality. Gordon's hothouse on the patio and Julie's studio in the extra bedroom were their retreats. Yet, they were able to come back together to share the creations and accomplishments of their alone time. This was the beginning of an intimate love relationship which endured three years. They were two vital, independent people who complemented each other. Unbound by roles and ruts, they were able to expand in many directions. They didn't seem to need a specific commitment on paper. Their caring and vibrancy seemed to insure their tomorrows.

As Julie and Gordon grew personally, professionally and as a couple, they became acutely aware of how enriching their time together was. They were supportive of each other's careers, shared in the responsibilities of household management, and introduced new and exciting ways and ideas into their lives. As the relationship matured they decided on a family. However, their Parent tapes dictated that they must first marry and own their own home.

Just before taking those steps to the altar, their first serious disagreement occurred. Gordon had taken it for granted that Julie would take his name and was shocked that she was considering keeping her maiden name. Flushed, he yelled, "You're going to be my wife. This isn't practice, it's for real!" Julie became Mrs. Gordon Baines.

They spent their honeymoon moving into a large colonial style home. Julie insisted that a large house was not only a wise investment, but would also give their family room to grow. Gordon had been uneasy over the amount of the mortgage payments, but as he moved crates and boxes about he began feeling the joy of owning *his* own home. Parent tapes began playing as he proudly hung a brass plaque on the front door, "Mr. & Mrs. Gordon W. Baines, Jr." As he screwed the plaque into the door he wondered if his Dad felt the same way when he bought his first house.

A few months in the big house taught him to expect the unexpected — more repairs and more bills. Although he didn't occasionally mind playing the master plumber, he was angry and resentful over all the unexpected bills and demands on his time. Each month the pressure mounted as he went over the check stubs.

Julie was growing irritable over Gordon's attitude. "Cooking had always been a time of sharing for us. We'd have fun joking and talking while we concocted some unique dishes. Suddenly he won't even wash a spoon! He's constantly complaining about how many clients he had to see or that he needs time to work with his plants. It's as if I don't have a demanding job!"

Anger churning in his gut, Gordon bellowed, "Julie's always screaming and nagging at me. I'll never get over her buying that new couch. Doesn't she realize the financial responsibilities *I'm* carrying with this monstrosity of a house she had to have? Her salary is only a drop in the bucket! I'm doing my damnedest to be a good husband and take care of *my* wife, but she uses her artistic temperament as an excuse to buy, buy, buy!"

Julie spent more and more of her evenings alone in her studio while Gordon kept his nose stuck in legal briefs. If they weren't arguing, their conversations was ritualistic and sterile. Gordon wasn't aware that Julie was heading up an important research project with a breakthrough near at hand. Julie didn't know that Gordon was preparing a case that might eventually be heard in the State Supreme Court.

The disagreement which catapulted them into divorce court occurred when Gordon accused Julie of being frigid and that it was her fault she hadn't become pregnant. Hysterically Julie screamed, "I don't want to raise children with an overbearing man who thinks I'm just a maid and a sex object. I can't make love to a man who believes the sun rises and sets on him!" In a nasty superior tone he came back with, "My children don't need a mother who refuses to cook and prefers finger painting to a clean house!"

Gordon and Julie's story is all too common — living together successfully and marrying only to divorce shortly thereafter. They were able to retain strong individual identities in their living together relationship by not assuming traditional sex roles and by taking an interest in each other's hobbies and career accomplishments. No Parent tapes played because they had none for a living together arrangement.

With the words, "I now pronounce you man and wife," Parent tapes, sex role models and unverbalized expectations came to the fore. What worked when they lived together was no longer workable after they married. The pull of Gordon's Parent tapes and expectations about how a husband and wife *should* behave was too strong for him to overcome, and he reverted back to traditional cultural tapes about marriage. The result, as happens all too often, was divorce.

We again emphasize that the best way to prevent or solve this problem is through a personal relationship contract. The process of working through such an agreement would have brought each of their wants and expectations to the surface, thereby permitting them an opportunity to explore their options and work toward solutions.

REMARRIAGE

Nancy was an intelligent young woman whose life experiences didn't match her I.Q. Although by 19 she had completed two years of college, books hadn't prepared her to enter her first marriage as Robert's second wife and Bobby's stepmother.

Robert's first wife, Quinn, came from a well-to-do southwestern family. When it came to ranching, snow skiing or jet setting, Quinn was no tenderfoot. After the divorce she and her four-year-old son, Bobby, moved in with a ski instructor.

Being the impulsive, free spirited, get-with-it person she was, Quinn invited Robert and Nancy to spend Christmas holidays skiing with them. She convincingly argued, "After all, for Bobby's sake we can be one big happy family at Christmas time." Both Robert and Nancy were squeamish over the idea, but since the romantic ties had long since faded and Robert was eager to see his son, they accepted the invitation.

Over drinks the evening of their arrival, Quinn told Nancy it was foolish for her to have to pay an instructor for ski lessons. She insisted she would take Nancy on as her pupil.

Bright and early the next morning they left for the ski course. Since the slopes were literally crawling with holiday vacationers, Quinn suggested that they use a secluded trail, little known to the tourists. The lesson began, "Nancy, point your right ski as far to the right as you can and your left ski as far to the left as you can. Now push off with your ski poles." After an hour of making herself into a wishbone Nancy gave up, sat on her skis and scooted down to the bottom of the hill. Amidst Quinn's reassurances that learning to ski takes time, Nancy settled herself in at the ski lodge while Robert, Quinn and her lover skied for the rest of the day. Angry at what she figured must be her lack of ability and exhausted from her lesson, she napped until they returned. The next day's lesson was a repetition of the first. The third day she begged off.

The next year Nancy and Robert again went skiing, but this time alone and at a different resort. Nancy decided it was now or never, "I'll learn this time or give it up." Watching for a moment her instructor reassured her, "It's all right; you haven't been on skis before." Bristling, Nancy came back with, "Oh, but I have." After a few minutes of the most elemental instruction, a light went on in her head as she realized that Quinn had been teaching her to do everything backwards. Nancy had been initiated into second wifehood!

An estimated 1,128,000 divorces were granted in the U.S. in 1978. This represents a 3% increase over the number for 1977, 1,091,000. During the twelve month period ending August, 1979, 1,157,000 couples were divorced, 38,000 more than for the preceding twelve months. The divorce rate was 5.3% per 1,000, or 4% higher than the rate for the twelve months ending with August, 1978. Of the 63.2 million children under eighteen in 1978, 18.6% were living with one parent and 10.2% were living with one natural parent and one stepparent.[3]

Despite the increase in the number of divorces, more Americans are getting married and remarried than ever before. By 1975, remarriage accounted for nearly one quarter of all men's marriages as compared to one-seventh in 1960. The data for 1975 revealed that four out of every five divorced persons remarried by middle age. During the twelve-month period ending in August, 1979, there were 2,289,000 marriages, an increase of 69,000 over the twelve-month period

---

[3]*Vital Statistics Report 1979*, National Center for Health Statistics.

ending with August, 1978. The high rate at which the divorced remarry suggests disillusionment with a specific marriage, but certainly not with the institution of marriage. These statistics indicate that the two-parent family remains the preferred living arrangement for Americans.[4]

Nonetheless, the attitudes and services society provides for the divorced and remarried family are out of touch with today's realities. Maddox states, ". . . society has exchanged one unworkable idea for another. It has given up the belief of indissoluble marriage . . . but it has not given up the belief that an unbroken home is essential for a child's sound emotional development."[5] In her study of the remarriage family, Shirley Maxwell Jones concluded that with appropriate skill and training in coping with divorce, remarriage and parenting, adults and children need not experience remarriage as an unworkable experiment.[6]

Most people entering a second marriage are ill-prepared to handle the financial constraints and interpersonal complexities of relating to a new spouse, stepchildren, and the ever present ties to an ex-spouse and biological parent. A recent survey revealed that the basic problems in first marriages centered about immaturity, lack of readiness for marriage, and sexual difficulties. Children and money were ranked very low. Among reconstituted families, children and financial problems were given as the principal areas of conflict.[7]

In many instances, a second wife must work in order to keep the family's financial ship afloat. This kind of enforced employment needed to help support her husband's children and ex-wife can rain havoc on remarriage. When a second husband must contribute part of his income to help support another man's children, he may feel resentful and his new

[4]*Population Bulletin*, Vol. 32, No. 5, Feb. 1979.

[5]B. Maddox, *The Half Parent*, New York: Evans, 1975, pg. 174.

[6]Shirley Maxwell Jones, "Divorce and Remarriage: A New Beginning, A New Set of Problems," *Journal of Divorce*, Vol. 2, No. 2, Winter 1978.

[7]L. Messinger, "Remarriage Between Divorced People with Children From Previous Marriages: A Proposal for Preparation for Remarriage," *Journal of Marriage and Family Counseling*, Vol. 2, No. 2, 1976, pg. 193-199.

wife guilty for his having to do so. A further thorn in the side
of a second marriage is that second wives receive little credit
for rearing stepchildren and are often the target of anger,
resentment and misunderstanding from their own as well as
their stepchildren.

Society has yet to define positively the role and function
of a stepparent. Bohannon states, ". . . the American norm is
either to disregard the subject completely or that special care
be taken that no difference appears on the surface between
the stepparent and 'real' parenthood. Stepparents are not
'real' and the culture . . . provides no norm to suggest how
they are different."[8]

Being a stepparent is no easy feat. Not only does the
stepparent have to establish his or her role function and open
channels of communication and ways of relating to the children, he or she must also learn to share parenthood with the
biological parent. Shirley Maxwell Jones contends that a
stepparent has the right to be an equal partner in a parenting
relationship. She asserts that it is the responsibility of the biological parent to assist and support the new spouse in this
role and that the success of a stepparenting relationship depends not only upon the desire and ability of the stepparent
to assume the parental role, but also on the acceptance of this
role by the new spouse and children. There is yet another
variable affecting the success of a remarriage family. Regardless of a stepparent's desire and skill, and even with the support of the spouse, present social norms make it nearly impossible for a stepparent to parent completely.

Maddox alerts stepparents to cultural myths which make
stepparenting a formidable, if not exasperating task.

"A stepparent must not be cruel.
A stepparent must not usurp the place of a natural parent.
A stepparent must supply whatever elements of parenting
    a stepchild lacks or a spouse demands.
A stepparent must love the stepchild."[9]

---

[8]P. Bohannan, (Ed), *Divorce and After*, New York: Doubleday, 1970, pg. 119.
[9]B. Maddox, *The Half Parent*, New York: Evans, 1975, pg. 159.

SO YOU WANT TO BE A STEPMOTHER?

Surveys and research suggest the following:

1. If the new parent is a stepmother, the probability of the marriage surviving and marital happiness are reduced.

2. The role of the stepmother is considerably more difficult than that of the stepfather.

3. Stepmothers are less likely than stepfathers to achieve close ties with their stepchildren.

4. Because men do not have to deal with the myth of the "wicked stepfather," society is more supportive of their role and place in the home.

5. Regardless of her parenting skills, her stepchildren are likely to regard her with suspicion and distrust.

6. Much of a child's anger and resentment toward his or her father is projected onto the stepmother.

7. Stepmother-stepdaughter relationships present the greatest problems. In large measure this is a product of two women having to share the same man. Generally speaking, the older the daughter, the greater the difficulties. If the stepmother does not have open and firm support from her husband, and if the stepdaughter is allowed power and control over her stepmother, the family's chances for survival are poor.

8. Stepmothers are more likely to establish positive relationships with younger children regardless of their sex.[10]

EFFECTS OF REMARRIAGE ON CHILDREN

Older children have greater difficulties adjusting to a stepparent. If a child is over twelve at the time of the divorce or eight years or older at the time of remarriage, the likelihood of the youngster's developing emotional problems is

---

[10]Shirley Maxwell Jones. Ibid. pg. 221-222.

enhanced. Krantzler claims, "A parent's remarriage may prove more disruptive than a divorce, especially for adolescents. A teenager can usually appreciate the strains of a marriage and comprehend explanations of a divorce, but is less able to handle the hidden sexual and competitive jealousies that . . . a stepparent can arouse."[11]

Adolescents are argumentative, impulsive and self-centered. This derives from the fact that they are fighting to establish their own identities and place in the world. The presence of a stepparent can aggravate this very normal stage of development to the point of rebellious and even dangerous acting out. Firstborn children seem to possess greater readiness to perceive rejection and are therefore more sensitive and reactive to feelings of jealousy and competitiveness. It is not uncommon for the eldest child, particularly if he or she is an adolescent, to attempt to turn younger siblings against the intruder, the stepparent.

If a child is feeling intense anger or even hatred toward one or both biological parents, social sanctions prohibit direct expression of these feelings. As a result some stepparents are made scapegoats for the anger, hostility and antagonism felt toward a natural parent. A child's adjustment to a parent's remarriage is also related to the way his natural parents communicate their feelings about the divorce, their attitudes toward one another, and the pressures that are brought to bear upon the child to reject the other parent.

Since children are a direct link to the ex-spouse, they are subject to a wide array of overt as well as covert feelings, attitudes and pressures emanating from the adults in their lives. These same influences flow in the opposite direction, from children to parents. Unless children feel free to establish affectionate ties with all the significant adults in their lives, feelings of divided loyalties and the threat of abandonment for establishing these bonds are likely to exist.

If these problems aren't enough, newly remarried couples tend to avoid confrontations with each other. It is as if they have been burned once before, so they attempt to hide

---

[11]Mel Krantzler, *Creative Divorce*, New York: New American, Feb. 1975, pg. 189.

and deny whatever difficulties they have, so as not to cause another explosion. If they are effective in their avoidance techniques, it is inevitable that normal anger, wounds and resentment will grow, fester and come to the fore with a resounding explosion. When stored feelings have been kept under wraps for lengthy periods, they are extremely difficult to defuse. This is one of the reasons that second marriages are shorter lived than first marriages.

Notwithstanding these potential pitfalls, children and adults are better off when an unsuccessful marriage is dissolved and replaced by a better one. Although the divorce rate for remarriages is higher than for first marriages, the success of second marriages that *endure* is approximately the same as that for first marriages.[12]

MANIKINS

Eva, a tall, sharp-featured, attractive 15-year-old, has a stately, almost sphinx-like quality about her. The first time we met, she stood several arm lengths away, avoided eye contact and was cool and aloof. It was as if she viewed us as store window manikins rather than as real people. After exploring Eva's past it became clear why she perceived people, especially adults, as unfeeling and noncaring.

When she was seven her parents divorced. Eva's mother relinquished custody to her Father and never saw her again. Her Dad remarried the next year and Eva was elated over being part of a "real" family again, a father, stepmother and stepbrother. Her father adopted Tommy, so Eva felt she had an honest to goodness and forever little brother. She and her brother were so preoccupied building their treehouse and so excited over the impending birth of the new baby, that the summer flew by.

Not long after the baby was born, Eva began feeling like a fifth wheel. Her stepmother was either caring for the infant, helping her brother, or fighting with her dad. Her father had little time for her. Eva became frightened. She knew some-

---

[12]Shirley Maxwell Jones, Ibid. pg. 222-224.

thing was wrong and felt left out and alone. She was afraid to talk to her dad because, in her head, saying what you felt led to arguments, and she associated arguing with divorce and the disappearance of her mother. She kept her feelings bottled up.

When she was ten her dad and stepmother divorced. After the fighting over money, possessions and child support was over, her stepmother, adopted brother and half sister left, never to see Eva again. Shortly thereafter Eva made her childhood decision — not to trust, love or be close to anyone ever again.

Fearful of expressing herself honestly, she became manipulative and conning. This behavior, based on her decision not to trust, caused considerable conflict between Eva and others. Her sneakiness, lying and conning taught her peers not to trust her. The kids at school retaliated, which served to validate Eva's decision — don't trust or be close.

Her first meeting with her second stepmother-to-be was a chilling occasion. Eva withdrew making up poems in her head:

> "Another Mother we will see,
> What will happen to number three?"

Her second stepmother couldn't win for losing. If she punished her, Eva went to her father with tales of the wicked stepmother. If they went shopping together, her father got a penny by penny report of his wife's financial irresponsibility and overspending. Even when her stepmother was on the phone, Eva made innuendos about who might really be on the other end of the line. She constantly pitted one parent against the other. When her stepmother finally gave up on Eva, her husband accused her of being a bad mother. Enraged she told him he kept his head buried in the sand when it came to *his* daughter. Right or wrong the fight was on and divorce seemed imminent. Fortunately they sought family counseling.

In the first meeting with the family, Eva's isolation and standoffishness were immediately apparent. She only permitted a small piece of herself to show through and in turn let only a small portion of others past her wall. After three years the sum total description of her stepmother was, "She works for the same company as my Dad." She gave the impression that people were disposable objects who are here today and gone tomorrow.

During the latter part of the fourth family session, and for no apparent reason, Eva became excited and her words came tumbling out rushed and disjointed. She described a series of events which took place soon after the family moved back into the city from an outlying town. Unknown to anyone, Eva had learned of her natural mother's remarried name. Upon arriving in the city, she immediately looked the name up in the phone directory and found two listings. As suddenly as she began, she stopped. After several minutes of silence we asked if she had called. Eva looked surprised and answered, "Oh no, I wouldn't have known what to say."

She went on to tell us of the second incident which occurred several months later. "I was shopping for school clothes last summer when I saw my first stepmother. She was standing by the cosmetic counter and when she saw me she put on sunglasses so I wouldn't recognize her." The third incident occurred only a day before the family session. She had heard about a boy in her school who had the same name as that of her adopted brother. Although she hadn't seen him she learned that he, like her brother, was a blond. Excitedly she said, "I'm going to see if I can find him. I bet he's my brother!" With that, she again reverted back into her shell of cold indifference.

The fact that she related these events, and her animation in doing so, indicated that a part of her still yearned for contact with her earlier roots. Her ambivalence was reflected by her volley of words followed by periods of silence. This behavior indicated that her wish for closeness lay alongside her fear of rejection.

Eva's manipulativeness, detachment and interpersonal conflicts were directly related to the traumatic abandonments she experienced as a child and preteen. This could have been avoided or minimized had her father been sensitive to and invited the frightened youngster to share her feelings. His three marriages taught her that people can be replaced.

The accuracy of this impression was validated by study of her father's tapes, life script and behavior. His present wife's chief complaint was that no matter how hard she tried she couldn't make contact with or get to know him. His "don't be close" was a major reason for the failure of his marriages. If he learns to give up this attitude, the chances for survival of the marriage and his daughter's emotional well-being are good.

THREE TIME LOSER

Tricia couldn't believe that Roger was so underhanded and cruel, and she felt stupid for taking so long to figure out that he was having an affair. Tears and threats failed to pull her third marriage back together. She had to face it — it was over and done with. Barely able to catch her breath between sobs, she asked herself, "Why me, a three time loser?"

Her question could be answered by looking at her history and early childhood decisions. The men she chose for lovers and husbands had similar characteristics. Their behaviors were like echos from the past. Abandonment was the key.

All three of her husbands abandoned her, but in different ways. Roy, her first husband, was into drugs and alcohol. If he couldn't pop it, shoot it, or drink it, he didn't want it. He went on binges for days and even weeks at a time. He ended up permanently missing.

Determined not to go through this again, she looked for a person as different from Roy as she could find. While on the surface she hit the mark, like radar, her unconscious script decisions about herself and people zeroed in on another Roy. Bill, her second husband, wasn't a drinker or doper: he was a workaholic. As a cancer researcher, he spent his evenings and weekends in the lab. Bill abandoned Tricia for his work.

Lewis, her third husband, didn't fit either category. He wasn't a drinker, doper or workaholic. He was a womanizer. They began their affair while Tricia was in the midst of her second divorce and Lewis was still married to his second wife. This time she knew it would work. Eighteen months after their marriage, he left her for another woman.

A glimpse at Tricia's family background will help in understanding the development of her script, her choice of husbands and her ideas about how a wife should be treated.

Tricia's dad was a typical, hard working, top level executive who was married to his desk and that perpetual pile of papers he shuffled about from place to place. Her mother had been unhappy as a child and during adolescence became seriously depressed. Her mother's low self-esteem was reinforced by her husband's lack of attention. When Tricia was ten years old, her mother committed suicide. Tricia was left feeling angry and bitter — angry at her mother for deserting her and bitter at her father for his devotion to his work which she believed pushed her mother over the brink. She identified with her mother and decided that people couldn't be counted on.

Tricia's adult relationships, particularly with the opposite sex, reflected this decision. She seemed drawn to men who in one way or another left her. The hurt and pain she felt as a result of these losses left her feeling like her mother, depressed and questioning her self worth.

Tricia's Con, "I want a lasting intimate marriage," belied her ulterior belief, "You can't trust men!" She Responded by choosing men who fulfilled her prophecy. When they didn't change after marriage, she experienced their actions as a Switch. Her choice of men and the hurt and anger she felt indicated that the game was played to prove that men were undependable.

The fact of two unsuccessful marriages, both of which left her with the same psychological Payoff, should have alerted her not to enter into a third without first finding out the reasons for her choice of men. In Tricia's case, the only way to stop this repetitive cycle is to enter therapy, get in touch with her childhood decision, and make a new decision about her self worth and others.

DOORMAT

Kirby lay back on his couch, hands clasped behind his head, shoes off, relaxing after finishing a beer. Had he been observed by his ex-wife, she would have described him as, "a lazy arrogant s.o.b." Had he been observed by his second wife-to-be, she would have described him as, "a secure strong man in need of relaxation." Kirby was actually thinking about his upcoming marriage. What no one knew, not even Kirby, was that his second marriage would be a repeat performance of the first. Kirby hadn't changed, not one iota! Even though a few gray hairs were beginning to show, because he held onto his childhood decision about women, he still treated them the same — like doormats.

When Kirby was a young boy, his Mother sent him the message, "Be like Dad," and his dad taught him how. The kicker was that his dad was a rounder. Since script messages are sent verbally as well as non-verbally, and are incorporated into the little person with little or no Adult processing, the chances of conflicting thoughts, feelings and actions are high.

Kirby loved his mother but was confused. How could he be like his dad and still show his love for his mother? To do so would be contradictory! In order to be like Dad, the way Mom told him, he decided that men are superior and can do as they please. As an adult, he manifested this early and unconscious decision by treating women as though they were doormats.

Kirby grew up, married a girl like Mom and acted like Dad. So long as she was a good wife and mother and kept her head stuck in the sand, all went well and Kirby could live out his script. On those few occasions when his wife popped her head up out of the sand and asked, "Why are you fooling around? Did I do something wrong?" — all she got was silence. Kirby correctly read her questions as rhetorical, rather than as a demand for real answers.

Their marriage hobbled along for several more years until Kirby met the one and only. She even *waited* around for five years before Kirby decided to divorce his wife. Neither Kirby nor his new love saw what was actually happening. He was treating her like a doormat, and she was acting like one. By waiting for him, she stroked his sense of superiority and reinforced his childhood decision.

You can probably guess his Con and Switch. He'll profess his love and later pull the Switch by roving. More proof that women are doormats. Since she waited around for five years, it's a good bet she'll put up with him for another five before popping her head up to ask the same, though rhetorical, question, "Why are you fooling around?"

CAULIFLOWER EAR

Some men in our culture develop a boxer's mentality. They hear the bell, rise to the occasion, and retire at the end of the round until the next bell.

GONG: Sixteen-year-old Buddy notices that boys are acting differently towards girls and that girls are behaving differently toward him. Buddy puts away his bat and ball and adopts the 50's macho image complete with V8 engine, chopped top, lowering blocks and dual glass packs. Overnight he becomes a cross between Brando and McQueen. The girls love this dashing reckless male person with the slicked back D.A.

GONG: Buddy enters college. A crewcut replaces the D.A. and he dons the uniform of the day — khaki slacks with buckle in the back, button down collar, and white buck shoes. He's still dashing, but a bit more sophisticated. Instead of plying her with beer before trying to get in her pants, he speaks to her of Nietzsche, Thoreau and Van Gogh. He's exciting, titillating and stimulating.

GONG: After graduation he marries a girl in the sorority house down the street. Buddy's entry into the world of corporate life ignites his ambition. He focuses more and more on future goals, promotions, and his own key to the executive john. As future aspirations come into sharper focus, the present becomes blurred. His wife becomes a house frau, a showpiece for his business associates, and a bedtime diversion. From nine to five he is exciting, but at home he's a drag. His wife's complaints are clearly heard, but seldom acted upon. With threats of divorce, which would endanger his routine, life style and corporate image, he reluctantly agrees to see a marriage counselor. With six months of therapy and $1,200 behind him, he again becomes the old exciting Buddy. The new-found old Buddy stays around a couple of months before he withdraws back to his corner in front of the T.V.

GONG: His wife divorces him. Yelling foul because he didn't do anything to deserve this, Buddy adopts the "Hip, Honda and Hairy Syndrome " He turns in his suit for faded jeans, opens his shirt to the navel, and adorns himself with enough necklaces and chains to sink a battleship. He rediscovers girls, the twenty- to twenty-five-year-old variety, motorcycles, sports cars and the disco beat. Buddy is Hip! This attractive, exciting man in his late 30's is like meat on the hook for the right girl.

GONG: Buddy remarries. Within a year his pin stripes reappear. White shirts, ties and marketing reports are again the order of the day. Late night discoing turns into an occasional night out with too many drinks, a dance or two, and a roll in the nuptial sack.

GONG: Wife number two throws in the towel. Buddy is twice married and twice divorced. The marriage-go-round resumes.

Buddy's life style is reactive. His changes and promises to change are really in the service of protecting the status quo, and as such are short-lived. While his intentions may be honest, his behaviors tell us that his unconscious motives are different. Once he finds a woman who fits his wants and needs, he quickly falls back into old patterns. It is as if he made an early childhood decision, "I don't have to move until the bell rings." This is the ulterior motive behind the Con of excitement and vitality. Once married and settled in, he pulls the Switch by again becoming a stagnant bore.

If you are married to a true blue Buddy, you have one of two choices.

GONG: Stay or leave.

Now that you have read the game sections and have seen yourself in some of these gamey situations, you may be saying, "That's me, how do I change?"

There are three steps to change:

1. Awareness
2. A New Decision
3. Practicing the Decision

The awareness, "That's me," is the first step in change, but awareness in and of itself is not enough. Knowing your games and that others like you also play, may offer temporary relief, but if you don't alter this behavior, you are apt to place yourself back into the same or a similar position. For example, knowing you have an ulcer will relieve you of your fear of stomach cancer, but unless you know and take the steps to cure the ulcer you may end up just as dead.

Some of the hows of change can be accomplished through self-help and individual effort. Others require the aid of a therapist. Seeing a therapist doesn't necessarily mean you are mentally unbalanced. Many intact people enter therapy because of conflicts and behaviors they are unable to resolve by themselves. The crucial issue is obtaining a clearer picture of yourself in order to make new decisions, thereby preventing a replay of past errors and hurts.

Before entering a new business a good businessman looks at his skills and talents and the demands on his time, energy and financial resources and balances them against the estimated personal and financial rewards of the new venture. The result of this survey is a go/no go decision. If the decision is to proceed, the next step in the sequence is goal setting. Specific goals are set by weighing what he wants to accomplish against the realities of his time, energy, financial resources and the demand for the product or service. To enter a new venture or enterprise without going through this process is personally and financially irresponsible. Yet, the divorced who are also entering a new venture, a new life style, seldom use these ideas.

When a young couple gets married they plan ahead by charting their course and setting a time frame for children, a house, savings and the other things they want and expect of marriage. Like the businessman they set goals and priorities. Why shouldn't the divorced do likewise?

The sad fact is that after divorce most people don't perceive and identify themselves as single, don't make new decisions, and don't set goals which fit their new status. The result is that the divorced become so *reactive* to the many pressures and demands made upon them, that they become scattered and go off in a dozen or so different directions at the same time. Sooner or later they feel tossed about by people and circumstances and powerless to control their own destinies. The harder they work, the more energy they expend and the less they accomplish. Because they lack a plan, a viable set of goals, their hard work boils down to an inefficient expenditure of time and energy. All too often the result is anxiety, depression and lowered self-esteem.

The concepts of awareness, energy, goals and games are intimately related. Think of your energy reserves as consisting of a finite number of units, 100 per day. The question you must then ask yourself is, "Am I in charge of how, when and the number of units expended?"

Without a set of goals, you will expend your units haphazardly as you react to the forces and demands placed upon you by others. If you are aware, make new decisions and set goals, you will be in control of and can spend your units of energy whenever and with whomever you please, i.e., 40 units on you, 30 units on your children, 15 units on your ex, 5 units on your parents, and 10 units on a new relationship. Having identified how you expend your energy, you are in a position to reorder or prioritize them. You might decide that spending 15 units on your ex is too much and 10 units on new relationships is not enough.

If you expend your units reactively, you will feel impotent, out of control and therefore down on you and the world. As a result, your positve stroke reserve will become depleted and you will be more vulnerable to after divorce games. To avoid this trap, the divorced must establish short- and long-term goals. The net effect is that they are structuring and taking charge of their lives.

To this end, we have provided you with a list of probing questions. If, after studying the list, you still feel at an impasse and unable to take charge of you, we suggest you give yourself the gift of therapy.

Know You

1. What ego state do you typically behave out of? Is it different in social, family and work situations?
2. What is your Life Position?
3. Do you know the difference between your parents' wants and expectations of you (Parent tapes) and your Adult beliefs and values?
4. Are you aware of the significant childhood decisions that have molded your life?

5. What is your life plan (script)?
6. Do you know the difference between your needs and wants?
7. Are you aware of your personal stimulus value, the impression you convey to others?
8. Can you identify the after divorce games you typically play?
9. What are your usual ways of structuring time?
10. What kinds of holes do you feel in you and how do you plug them up?
11. Since your divorce, has your view of you and your world changed? How and to what degree?
12. Are you unhooked from your ex-spouse and the marital relationship?

Know Your Wants in a New Relationship

1. What qualities do you look for in another person? What about this person attracts you? Do you know why?
2. What roles and functions do you want the other to assume? Which will you assume?
3. What kinds of people do you typically seek out? What has been the outcome? To what extent does the newest person in your life fit this pattern?
4. Are you in hook love? If yes, after you engage your Adult ego state how will the relationship change?
5. Do you meet each others' emotional, familial, social and financial needs and wants? If not, is there room for compromise?
6. Are your philosophies of life and life styles compatible? If not, can a workable compromise be effected?
7. How do you usually feel after being with the person? Is this feeling familiar? If yes, does it take you back to another person, place or time?
8. Do you compare this person to your ex-spouse? In what ways?
9. Are your carrying bad feelings into your new relationship from your previous relationship or marriage?
10. Taking into account your scripts, tapes, life positions, ways you structure time and life styles, what is the proba-

bility that this relationship will be lasting and intimate?
11. What are your goals for this new relationship?
12. Are both you and your partner willing to make a written personal relationship contract?
13. How soon after your divorce or the breakup of a living together relationship did you enter into this relationship? Has it been too soon?
14. What were the real, not surface, conflicts you experienced in your previous marriage or relationship? Are you experiencing them in this relationship?

How Much and What Are You Willing to Give in a New Relationship?

1. What and how much of you are you willing to give to the new person and the relationship?
2. Do you feel hemmed in, drained and controlled by another? How and in what ways? Who is really in charge of you?
3. What are you willing to give up or compromise in order to keep the relationship?
4. Do you typically feel a loss of freedom and independence in a love relationship? If yes, are you choosing controlling people or operating out of a "don't be close" framework?

Your Willingness to be a Stepparent and Extended Family Member

1. How much energy are you willing to expend to become part of a blended and extended family?
2. To what extent are your willing to parent another person's children?
3. What are your expectations of your role and function as a stepparent? Have you communicated them to your new love?
4. Are you aware of your new love's wants and expectations of you as a stepparent? Are you in agreement with them?
5. Is your new love aware of your wants and expectations of him/her as a stepparent? Does he/she agree with them?
6. Has your role and status as a stepparent been clearly established and communicated to all? Has your partner's

role and status as a stepparent been clearly defined and communicated?

7. If either you or your new love has been rejected as a stepparent, have you worked out a strategy to deal with this?

8. Have you asked your children how they feel about you and your new love living together? If they object how will you deal with it?

YOUR TURN

Since the inception of our newspaper column five years ago, it has been our practice to answer every letter we receive. Each letter is carefully read and discussed. Frequently the opinions of other professionals are sought. In formulating our replies we keep in mind that oftentimes the writer is in the midst of crisis and therefore his Adult (clear, crisp thinking) is contaminated by his Child ego state (intense feelings). Contamination is evident in many of the letters.

While we do not attempt to solve anyone's problems in a letter, we do inject our own Adults into their situation in an effort to provide the writer with a clearer, more comprehensive picture of the problem. Armed with a clearer and perhaps different perspective, the writer, we hope, will be in a better position to think through and solve his own problem and, if necessary, seek the services of a therapist or attorney.

We are going to give you an opportunity to use what you have learned by sharing some of the letters we have received. These letters were chosen because of the diversity of problems and feelings expressed. Before reading them, we suggest you first read the game checklist we have devised which we use to analyze the letters into their essential elements. After reading a letter, decide on your reply.

We ask that you do this not as an exercise in amateur psychology, but rather, as an opportunity to practice your skills in divorce-related problems. By so doing you will learn to deal more effectively with your divorce and after divorce problems.

Game Checklist
1. What ego state is the writer in?
2. Has the writer assumed the position of:
   A. Rescuer
   B. Victim
   C. Persecutor
3. Is the writer describing a game transaction?
   A. Can you find a Con, Gimmick or Switch?
   B. What is the ulterior message?
   C. What do you think the Payoff will be?
   D. Is it a first, second or third degree game?
   E. Is it a single, double or multi-handed game?
   F. What would you name the game?
4. Can you make some inference about the writer's life position, script and Parent tapes?
5. Is the writer, if an ex-spouse, unhooked?
6. Is there something the writer can do to solve the problem or end the game?
7. If anger is expressed, is it aimed at the right target?
8. Are the writer's priorities appropriate, i.e., are the children in physical or emotional jeopardy while their parents take potshots at each other?
9. Is the person writing for someone else? If so, to what end?
10. What do you think the other side of the story would be?
11. What do you think will happen to the writer in the future?

*   *   *

To Whom It May Concern,

I have read several of your articles and hope you can help. I am seventeen, my parents have been divorced for nearly eight years, but you'd never know it. They still see each other and are nice to their ex-in-laws. Yet, my mother talks about my father like he's trash. My parents separated in 1972 and I lived with mom until 1978, when I came to live with my dad and his parents.

After the divorce my dad bought this home for my mom and I so we could get away from our ghetto. She still treats him like trash, yet lives in his home rent-free. She has threatened several times to go to court and get me back. I love her, but could never go back to her lies and self-pity. I can't take seeing my dad hurt. I'm *very* confused and *quite sick* of this game!

Please tell me what to do.

Sincerely,

Confused

* * *

After Divorce,

I'm just like any other father that wants his children nearby. I read Mr. Melvyn's statements in the newspaper and believe in the right of a man having his children as close to him as possible, married or not.

I also have the same problem. I have two children, ages three and seven, after living with this woman I once loved very much. Finding out she had another lover, I took actions which brought me here to the Arizona State Prison for five to ten years. Now the only thing I want is to be able to see my children. It isn't no trouble for my family to bring them to me, but their mother wishes not to. As far as they know I died. She wishes not to receive no mail or calls from me. I understand what has happened between us, but there is no reason for her to act this way on my communications with my children. If there is any way you can help me be free to do so.

Thank you.

* * *

Dear Melvyn A. Berke, Ph.D. & Joanne Grant,

I do not subscribe to the Houston Chronicle; I have to watch my pennies, and those that I do have seem better spent elsewhere. Occasionally, however, as was the case today, I buy a paper to read the houses for sale section and dream.

First of all, I will not deny that many ex-husbands are indeed the lousy stinking scum of the earth deserving of all the inhumane tortures that society can create. But, hey, wait a minute — couldn't there be another side to the story? I've never seen it in print — or on television — or heard it on the radio; but I have heard it in whispered tones in alleyways.

I know that neither you, nor anyone else in "power," gives a damn — but you are getting ready to hear the other side.

My ex-wife acted like a slut for four years (that I know of) and I more or less put up with it because of our two young boys. Finally, she met Mr. Future and, with the help of a shyster lawyer and a holier-than-thou judge took me to the cleaners for everything we owned. The judge was considerate enough to allow me to keep all the debts. She got the boys and everything else.

To pay child support, I cancelled each and every insurance policy (including automobile) I owned — who the hell could pay those premiums. I've lived like a second class citizen. Half of my furniture is homemade. My couch is so broken down Goodwill wouldn't have it. My car is twelve years old and has 146,000 miles on it. I could go on — but you get the idea.

My ex-wife remarried and she and her husband have a gross income of three or four times mine. Just in the past year, they've bought (according to my boys and my eyes), approximately $4000 worth of jewelry, a complete houseful of furniture, two new vehicles, three businesses, etc.

They spend most of their time beating my boys (leaving welts and bruises), arguing in front of the boys, belittling me (telling the boys what a lousy worthless lazy creep I am, etc.).

Oh sure, I could go back to court and get my child support reduced — if I could afford a lousy lawyer. That's a laugh! And what makes you think I'd get a fairer shake from the courts this time? Most of the lawyers and judges are as addle brained as you. How the hell do you get a change of venue from prejudiced judges? Yes, I pay child support — and no I've never been taken to court for nonpayment.

I work my ass off — and make just enough money to pay

my bills and the child support. I've never been able to afford anything extra. I'll never be able to save up enough for a down payment on a home of my own . . . or enough for a lawyer to fight the damn injustices done to the "ex-husband" — otherwise known as the worthless, stingy slob.

Worse yet, I've still got nine years of this misery to look forward to. By then, I'll be too old to have much of a second life.

Back to the child abuse. Don't tell me about reporting it to the authorities. I spent three hours one weekend trying to find someone in authority to listen to me. I must have been shunted from, to and between two dozen different people and as many organizations — none of which gave a damn. It just happened to be Labor Day weekend. By the time everybody returned to work and felt like listening, all the marks, etc. were healed and gone.

Nobody gives a damn — and you ain't any different.

Yes, I know, this letter could have been a hell of a lot more tactful. But, it would not have accomplished anymore. It will wind up in the trash can one way or the other. If for one second out of an eternity I thought it would do any good, I'd sign my name and address.

Phooey from me to you,

Anonymous

      Otherwise known as — the ex-husband
                         the worthless lazy slob
                         the stingy bastard
                         the sucker from 1975
                               (year I was divorced)
    and, as my boys call me, Daddy

*   *   *

Dear Dr. Berke and Joanne Grant,

My ex-wife initiated our divorce five years ago. In the settlement she got a sizable sum in cash, our house, a new car and ample child support. She has already gone through the cash and only worked about two years. My problem is the children are beginning to resent my life style, and I resent their having to do without things I once provided for them. What can I do?

*   *   *

Dr. Berke,

I wish your column would fail — your kind of articles are a disservice to the public. There is too much talk and writing material about divorce. What is wrong with good old marriage and the vows? How do you know so much about divorce — you must have left a wife and children.

You must be a sex fiend.

Mrs. John Doe

P.S. I bet you tell men and women to have sex if they aren't divorced.

* * *

Dear Dr. Berke and Joanne Grant,

My husband was the one who wanted our divorce. At first I was against it, but since we have been unhappy for more than three years and what we were doing wasn't working, I agreed. Things will be final in three weeks so I was shocked when he called last night asking for a reconciliation.

I just cried, and he kept talking. I don't think I want to go back to him, but if I don't why did I cry? I have behaved normally until now and haven't even cried. What's happening to me?

* * *

Dear After Divorce Editors,

I suspected my husband was cheating on his family . . . then in November he moved out, after cancelling marriage counseling three times.

Our children are four and seven years old. On his first visitation he took them to his ex-secretary's house, shared her bed and played house. The children were totally confused. The gutless wonder didn't even have the courage to tell me; he let our daughters tell me about "Daddy's girlfriend."

Now the problem: The woman hides her eyes and pretends to cry because, "You like your Mommie better than me." When they came home they said they were told to call the woman's parents "Grandma & Grandpa." My ex-husband doesn't seem to realize the confusion and frustration he is causing our children . . . or it's his way of getting back at me.

We are Catholic, the girls go to catechism and church, then they spend time with him and it is a contradiction of everything they are taught. I am boiling, confused and very upset!

Yes, I dislike the "other woman" being a substitute mother and mothering my children, particularly when I learned she had been playing around with my husband for about a year. Yes, I dislike my ex-husband for neglecting the kids and me and making his own little world. Should I have his visitation rights cut down?

Sincerely,

*   *   *

Dear Dr. Berke and Joanne Grant,

My daughter misbehaved and asked me not to tell her father. He has been a good parent since our divorce. When I asked why she said, "He wouldn't think of me as Daddy's little girl any more."

It's been a long time since she has been a little girl and I'm concerned about her fantasy and behavior.

*   *   *

Dear Dr. Berke and Joanne Grant,

My 15-year-old daughter resents the men I see to the point where I won't invite a man into our home. I have been divorced five years but because of her attitude I rarely date. Her father works for an oil company overseas so they seldom see each other, though he writes a couple of times a month. She just stays mad but won't talk about it. Any ideas?

*   *   *

Dear Dr. Berke and Joanne Grant,

I am writing this letter in the hopes others won't mess up like I did. For the past six years I have hassled with my ex-husband trying to get him to pay child support. He has given me a million-and-one excuses and promises to pay, but never does. Over the years I must have threatened him with court at least a dozen times but I never did anything about it. On our last go-around we agreed, in the presence of our lawyers, to reduce the amount owed from $9,000 to $5,000 if he would pay for our son's orthodonture work.

This morning, some five months and zero dollars later, I took him to court. When the judge asked him his plans for paying the back support, he said he hadn't thought about it. The judge told him he could arrange some thinking time and ordered a 72-hour think session in jail.

Since he was supposed to take our son to the orthodontist later that afternoon, I asked the judge not to jail him. The judge disagreed saying my ex wouldn't follow through and that I should be realistic and forceful.

Guess what? I let him off the hook and he never took our son to the orthodontist. For once I had a judge, lawyer and the system on my side and I blew it. I wanted to believe my fantasy. We are scheduled for a follow-up hearing next month, and I hope they put him in Sing Sing.

* * *

Dear Dr. Berke & Joanne,

I feel divorced for all intents and purposes. I am almost 25, got married on my 24th birthday and my ex-wife was 19. We split up after eleven months of marriage. Basically, the marriage went down because of too much influence from her mother in our lives, lack of cooperation on her part to put energy into keeping the marriage together and the influence (bad) of an old boyfriend. I found out later through a friend of ours (female) that Julie was seeing this guy before we split up.

I am curious, what percentage of marriages break up because of infidelity when the wife is to blame (as mine obviously was)? Also, what is the general opinion on whether or not one should meet other companions after a separation that will inevitably lead to divorce?

I would like to know these answers and also the results of your survey as I am interested in how others deal with this social problem.

Thank you very much . . .

Sincerely,

* * *

Dear Sirs:

In a recent Ann Landers column, a woman writer asked if all men cheat on their wives and Ann stated that 40% of men married less than 7 years "stray." After that 70% do. At about age 55 it drops to approximately 50% and tapers off from there on. If this estimate is correct then there must be this many women cheating too! My thoughts run wild!

I am still single following my divorce 16 years ago. I am not opposed to marriage but find that most people just want to play around and not be committed to only one mate!

After my divorce, I tried dating and had no problem finding men but most all of them wanted to play games. For instance most of them had 2 or 3 other women "on the string" and the rest had a jillion excuses why they could not enter into matrimony. All of them blamed their ex-wives for their divorce! All the men I dated wanted a live-in arrangement but were adamant about their ex-wives not doing the same.

In my 16 years of being around men I have come to the conclusion that a man does not necessarily have to have an unhappy situation at home to cause him to be adulterous!

* * *

Dear Dr. Berke and Ms. Grant,

After spending the past eight years living with a man I'll call John, I am beginning to question the relationship. I am 30 years old. My 9-year-old son looks on John as his dad.

Getting married didn't concern me very much so I haven't pressed the issue, much to the dismay of my relatives and some friends. Having been through an unhappy divorce John uses the excuse of being afraid, "marriage would ruin our relationship," but I feel he wants to avoid any financial liability in case of divorce.

I feel insecure in the relationship the way it stands. We are buying a lovely home and car and another car is paid for. All are in his name. We have owned and sold three successful businesses in which I have participated with long hours of hard work. These businesses (and checking accounts) are in his name, "to avoid problems in case of bankruptcy." Our personal checking account is in both our names, but not the savings account. He has a life insurance policy naming me as beneficiary.

I am worried that in case of his death his parents, a sister or his previous wife and son would be able to step in and take away what I think is equally mine. We have no wills. Is this a realistic fear?

I am also concerned that he may tire of me as I grow older and want out of the relationship. Will I have any legal recourse to my contribution through the years?

In what way will our living together affect our Social Security benefits in later years? In the past I have either spent my time running our business or being "wife" and mother so my contribution to my own Social Security fund has not been significant.

What steps would you advise I take to insure success and more security either within my relationship with John or on my own?

Sincerely,

*   *   *

Dear Melvyn Berke and Joanne Grant:

At first my intention was to write for your written words entitled *"After Divorce"* — solely. But, I would like to tell you a few things. I'm in the midst of a no-fault divorce after 16 years of marriage. I truly enjoy y'all's column in Tuesday's paper. Just about every article hits home with me — in another typical divorce situation.

I didn't marry until age 31 after having four fantastic years in college and an exciting and wonderful eight-year career as an airline stewardess. I met many people, dated many men, fell really in love only once. This is not the man I married — but I thought the man I did marry would be perfect for me. Everything I do has to be done "right" and complete — that is the way I am. After five years of marriage we adopted children — I also wanted to be the "best" mother — so I allowed myself the joy and luxury of being a fulltime mother.

Not having the desire to maintain a good sexual relationship with my husband, he didn't press me, so I never brought up the subject. He didn't woo me — I didn't care (I'd been wooed by many a man). I just wasn't *in love* — but I *cared* about this man. Then eventually he wrote me a 10-page letter telling me everything I do wrong and two paragraphs of what I *try* to do right. He said I *overdo* everything, etc. Things that were physically correctable, that irritated him and were nothing off my back to do and yet allowed me to still be *me* — the *same* person I was 16 years ago, I corrected immediately.

To make a long story short — I have done *everything* humanly possible to make this man care again and if I could *hand* him the moon he would say, "Damn it! You brought it in the *wrong hand!*"

Thanks,

P.S. I hope you personally read my note rather than a secretary merely opening it and sending the booklet — without you ever reading *my words.*

* * *

Dear A.D.

I am a 39-year-old male who is in the process of getting a divorce from my spouse of 16 years. My biggest problem is I am an alcoholic and it took separation to wake me up after I was cited for a DWI in December. Two weeks later I enrolled in AA and they have helped me enormously as I now have a place to go and people to see and talk with. My wife is quite overweight and has a position of tremendous responsibility with a great firm. At her job she is thought of as the best thing since bubble gum. She says I turn her off because when she comes home I complain that she does not cook, clean house properly, wash clothes at regular times, etc.

My question is: I love my wife so should I seek help from the clergy or just say it's all over but the rent. I've tried to talk with her calmly but it is always a fast argument. What do you suggest I do? I know I was wrong but does she know that she was too?

Thanks,

* * *

Dear Dr. Berke & Joanne Grant,

My husband and I have been legally separated for about two years, because we just couldn't get along together. We get along better since we are apart, and the children are crazy about their father. The judge told him to pay child support for our four boys. He set the price at $200.00 a month, but he has never given it to them, not once. I hate to have them pick him up because the children love him so much, but it's really hard to support four boys and myself and take care of all the bills. Could you please give me some kind of advice on getting child support. Please answer soon.

*   *   *

Dear Dr. Berke & Joanne Grant,

I have been reading your article, After Divorce, hoping to find a solution to this problem. We are grandparents married 50 years. Our son was divorced 2 years ago after 20 years of marriage. A divorce he did not want. His good friends on the job introduced him to an attractive, talented, seemingly intelligent woman six years older than he. We thought how lucky for him. He has four children and sends the youngest $300 a month support. The other three are supporting themselves. Right after he was married his new wife made it clear to his children that they were busy and didn't know when they would have time for them.

My grandson's wife and I cooked a birthday dinner for their grandfather. Their dad was invited and he said they would come. I called a couple of days before and in a very nasty voice she told me they would stop by on their way to the theater.

We have a wonderful relationship with our grandchildren. When our son was transferred East, he did not call or see his children before he left. They were very hurt. We cannot understand why he does not take a stand and let her know these are nice kids and would not bother her.

One of our granddaughters is getting married next Sunday. She has written twice to her Dad asking him if he would come and give her away. He never answered. No gift or anything. We are humiliated, embarrassed and sick over this. I think sometimes our son would have been better off to have picked somebody off the streets with compassion.

I am not an interfering in-law but her ex-husband lives 100 miles from us and I would like to talk to him and ask him some questions about her. It seems like money means more than anything else to her. I wish I didn't feel this way.

Hoping you will read this,

Sincerely,

*   *   *

Dear Dr. Berke and Joanne Grant:

I was reading your column on divorce and it came to me you might be able to help me. You see, I have a son 34 years old who is one of my five children. He got a divorce over a year ago from a woman who couldn't be true to anyone if she tried. She got married the next day after the divorce. Now I hear that the marriage is on the rocks and she wants my son back. She lives in another state and calls him three or four times a week collect ... sweet talks him. He has an eleven-year-old daughter who he loves very much and is thinking about going back to her for his daughter's sake. They really didn't have a good marriage but they had a lot ... two new cars, new house, lots of clothes, a good job but he was never enough for her in the sex department.

She hated his family. He could never write, call or come to see us but once a year and then she would start an argument an hour after they got here and she would say, "Lets go home" and he would follow her like a puppy dog. Her mother told me once he really missed us so I know he must have feelings for us. Now he is turning against all of us again since he is talking to her and thinking of going back to her.

He is a very shy person and hasn't gone out to find another woman. He doesn't know how to talk to them ... his wife is pushy and domineering, that is the reason he got in with her. He talks all the time of suicide as his ex-wife plays games. One week she will return to him then the next week tells him of the kinky ways her new husband and her have sex. We all think she is crazy and she is getting him crazy. I tried to talk him into going to a doctor but he said he isn't crazy and won't consent to it.

My husband and I aren't young anymore and we can't take all this worry. I am so afraid he will go through with the suicide or go back with her and she will do it all again to him.

Do you have any suggestions about what we can do? He blames me for everything and anything that has ever happened in his life. He blames me for his shyness, his marriage, his schooling ... you name it he blames me. I told him I was shy too but you got to help yourself get out of it. He doesn't try. I don't know where to turn. It would kill me if he ever went through with his suicide plans and I never did anything to help him. Please, if you know of anything I could do let me know.

Thank you,

P.S. She gets $50.00 a week for one child (support) and the new car, and all the new furniture. They sold the house and she talked him into giving her all the money for their daughter's sake. She uses the daughter to get anything and everything she wants. I would need 20 pages to tell you everything. Hope you can understand this writing.

*   *   *

Dear Dr. Berke & Joanne Grant,

What is the best way to handle this situation? My son and his wife were recently divorced. He is paying child support for their two children — she was awarded the children by mutual agreement. He pays her $300.00 per month which is over half of his earnings — he loves his children.

Prior to the divorce his children loved him — perhaps more than they loved their mother. They also loved us, their grandparents. We took care of the children much of the time.

Since the divorce she has turned the children against their father and against us. The children will have absolutely nothing to do with us. We send them birthday cards and Christmas gifts, but there is no acknowledgement.

Shall we try to forget them (this seems impossible) and just go on living?

It worries us what her attitude will do to the children.

*   *   *

Dear Dr. Berke & Joanne Grant:

My ex-husband introduced me to his bride-to-be. I like her. I'm sure she isn't aware that I left my (then) husband because of his violent temper and the beatings I received. Before we were married, I saw only the charming facade I'm sure she knows. His brother beat his ex-wives, severely, also. I'm talking about fractured bones — not just a slap in the face.

I feel that part of the problem preceded the marriages — both men truly hate their mother and feel dominated by her. However, my ex refused any sort of therapy and I got out!

I doubt that an ex-wife's words would be taken seriously, but should I warn this young woman or just let her experience the horror herself?

*   *   *

Dear Dr. Berke & Joanne Grant:

I am single, and am not looking for marriage in the near future, so it may seem odd that I'm writing to you. Here's the problem:

I have recently met a good, gentle man who is divorced. The divorce happened about a year and a half ago, but he is having many troubles. He loved his wife dearly, did all he could to prevent her leaving, and he still loves her. He feels guilty about having relationships with other women, friendly or sexually. He is hurt and confused. He can't let anybody get close.

I want to help him — I know it's his battle, but I also feel he needs someone to understand him. He is ready and willing to try, but I don't know what to do. Could you please help us?

*   *   *

Dear Dr. Berke and Joanne Grant:

I read your articles in the Sacramento Union and am hoping you can help my husband and I find a couple of answers regarding his seven-year-old daughter, Gina, from a previous marriage.

First, we have been having problems concerning a regular visitation schedule — especially for summer vacations. We would like to have Gina for at least a month and we are meeting with great resistance from her mother. Her reasoning being she feels it is too long for Gina to be away from her at this age — which is very interesting since she has been sending her to her grandmother's for two weeks every summer since she was 4 or 5. Do you have an opinion as to the length of time the average "divorced" child should be allowed to spend with her real father? I realize that every child is an individual and each case must be judged separately, and we are more than willing to have the matter reviewed by an expert.

Secondly, the mother has just recently remarried — at first we thought this would make things a lot better for everyone — but it was short-lived. The problems we are dealing with in this particular instance are:

1. When the mother remarried they had Gina stand between them, and when the new husband gave her mother the ring, he also gave Gina a ring. Gina now thinks that she is married to him and tells everyone this.

2. In my latest conversation with Gina's stepfather, he made it very clear that they have told Gina that she is his child and that he is her "real" father — and that now she has two daddies.

Although I feel Gina should be able to call her stepfather Daddy if that is her choice, it concerns me that she is going to be one confused little girl with their interpretation of the new relationship.

I would appreciate very much hearing your opinion, and am enclosing a self-addressed stamped envelope for your convenience in replying.

Sincerely,

* * *

Dear Dr. Berke & Joanne Grant:

This past Christmas my ex-husband put his girlfriend's gifts to our children under my tree. Every time I saw them lying there I got mad. I think his girlfriend could have arranged her gift-giving at his house. Please print this for girlfriends who intrude on another's family.

* * *

Dear Dr. Berke and Joanne Grant:

I am married to one of those fathers who pays child support regularly every month. His ex-wife is, and has been, on welfare for many years even though she is able to work and the kids are in school. As a matter of fact, she has two businesses on the side. At one time she lived in a more expensive house than we. You needn't suggest the Welfare Fraud Hot Line, because I have called with little success.

I would love to see what she does with my husband's money, since it isn't all spent on the kids. We also contacted the Child Protection Agency, because the children's clothes literally stunk and their stomachs were swollen from eating improperly. We have tried to get custody, but to no avail since proving unfit motherhood is next to impossible.

Why don't agencies investigate the legitimacy of child support and where it really goes rather than just making sure it comes out of the father's pocket? How about seeing which parent is best suited to take care of children both emotionally and financially?

*　　*　　*

Dear Doctor,

I was wondering if you might know something about a situation like this: My husband has been previously married and has two daughters by that marriage. They married at 17 and by the time they split, age 23, they had another child. My husband worked 5 jobs at once, and continues to work just as hard now. He is a good provider. His wife, apparently, started drinking and wouldn't get out of bed til' late afternoon. By this time the kids were in kindergarten and first grade. Bob, my husband, often had to take the kids to the bus and cook breakfast. At night, being there was no dinner, he had to take the kids out to eat. They finally split after 6 years of marriage.

She got a good lawyer, he a not-so-great one. She won custody of both girls with Bob getting reasonable visitation rights. He *never* got to see the kids again after they were divorced. The kids were 5 and 6 then, and adored their father. Before the divorce he took them all over including Disneyworld (an unforgettable experience for any kid). They are now 11 and 12 and young ladies. They were very bright girls and my question is: Could it be possible that their mother (Bob's ex) brain washed them into believing he deserted them or even worse, is dead? His ex has allowed the children *no* contact what-so-ever with any of Bob's family. Do you think the kids could forget about their father who had loved them (and still does) so much? He still buys them bonds on birthdays and is depressed around those times. His wife is still an alcoholic.

Any answer would be *so* appreciated —

Thank you

*   *   *

Dear Dr. Berke & Joanne Grant,

Please help me! I was divorced and remarried six years ago. This second marriage was fine until my teenage son came to live with us two months ago. His father threw him out of his house because of constant fights and low grades. He is fifteen. My present husband has two girls from his previous marriage. Both are married.

He was very willing to take my son in but it is painfully obvious that he resents him very much. Never talks to the child. Never a good thing to say about him. My son is on his best behavior, minds us, tries to be helpful and his grades are up.

Please help me. Tell me how to handle this situation. I want the three of us to be happy.

Thank you so much.

*   *   *

Dear Dr. Berke & Joanne Grant,

My husband of eight years has children from a previous marriage who live with their mother — also happily remarried. His son has integrated himself into our family quite nicely. His daughter, however, still shows signs of bitterness and resentment toward me. Through the years, I have tried to win her over, but nothing seems to change her feelings toward me. Have you any helpful information to offer regarding this frustrating situation?

Thank you.

*   *   *

How do you think your replies to these letters would be received? Now, write your own letter and answer to your after divorce problems. Would you take your own advice?

INDEX